THE WILDE LEGACY

The Wilde Legacy

Eiléan Ní Chuilleanáin

EDITOR

FOUR COURTS PRESS

Published by
FOUR COURTS PRESS LTD
7 Malpas Street, Dublin 8, Ireland
email: info@four-courts-press.ie
http://www.four-courts-press.ie
and in North America by
FOUR COURTS PRESS
c/o ISBS, 5824 N.E. Hassalo Street, Portland, OR 97213.

ISBN 1-85182-654-8

A catalogue record for this title
is available from the British Library.

Printed in Great Britain
by MPG Books, Bodmin, Cornwall

Contents

Contents

Illustrations

CREDITS
6 National Library of Ireland; 3 Royal College of Surgeons;
2 Eoin O'Brien

Acknowledgements

I would like to thank Oscar Wilde's grandson Mr Merlin Holland for kindly agreeing to act as patron of the conference on 'The Wilde Legacy'. I would also wish to acknowledge the generous support of the 'University of Dublin Fund', a fund supported by US-based alumni and friends of Trinity College Dublin, and the help given by Mary Apied and Daniel McGowan of the Trinity Foundation. The conference was given its shape by the energy of Nicholas Grene and Gerald Dawe of the School of English, and of Davis Coakley, then Dean of the Faculty of Health Sciences, and David McConnell of the School of Genetics, Trinity College. The session on 'Wilde in the Theatre' was recorded and transcribed by Denis O'Brien. Special thanks are due by the editor to Gerald Dawe and Nicholas Grene for advice, to Ruth Hegarty, Marie Glancy and the Oscar Wilde Centre for assistance, and to Fionnuala Dillane for invaluable editorial help.

Introduction

This book begins with the place where Oscar Wilde was born. Late in 1997, the house at No. 21 Westland Row, the first home of William and Jane Wilde, began a new phase of its existence. It had, like most of that side of the street, belonged to Trinity College for a number of years. Trinity's School of English was establishing a base for postgraduate teaching which had long needed a proper home. Studying for the Master's degree in Anglo-Irish Literature or for the new Master's in Creative Writing, students came from a variety of countries, and a variety of academic and non-academic backgrounds. The plaque on the façade commemorating the birth of Oscar on 16 October 1864 was joined by a neat wooden board in Irish and English announcing the Oscar Wilde Centre for Irish writing.

The College wished to commemorate and claim a famous former student. The School of English was expanding its teaching into creative writing and also wanted to open its activities to an outside audience. An international series of lectures and readings was held to mark the birth of the Centre. We began to plan a conference for the centenary of Oscar Wilde's death. In setting this up we felt (I claim credit by association as I was then Head of the Department of English) that the Wildes, for whom literature was never cut off from other human concerns, were being aptly remembered.

The main West Front of Trinity is all eighteenth-century grandeur, triumphantly facing the home of the old Parliament it has outlasted, and the statues of its own political and literary heroes. At the east end, facing Westland Row, there is quite a different architectural and academic mixture, the grand buildings named after the business benefactors of the late twentieth century, and the old houses not uncomfortably sandwiched, a mix of subjects too – mathematics, Women's Studies, creative writing and Irish writing. From 1997, No. 21 quickly grew – as such houses do – its own student-centred atmosphere, people of various ages drinking coffee and staring at the ceiling and working in corners, classes in the daytime. It remained itself, narrow and tall in a characteristically Dublin style, a little grim in its outlook, steadfastly confronting the dull integrity of the street, where purposeful teenagers carrying musical instruments dodged past the railway station and the commuters to find the door that opens on the hidden magnificence of the Royal Irish Academy of Music; where tourists in new raingear plodded towards Merrion Square and the National Gallery. Out of sight but very near were the back entrance of the College and the sites of the hospitals where William Wilde had worked and studied.

When, with the imminence of the centenary of Oscar Wilde's death in Paris, on 30 November 1900, our ideas for a commemorative conference were taking shape, that neighbourhood and that mixture of Dublin traditions of art, learning, medicine, politics and family life were influential in deciding that we should celebrate Oscar in the context of his family. We were lucky in being able to bring the connection into the very moment, as his grandson Merlin Holland was persuaded to open the proceedings. The present collection of essays is based on the doings of that weekend.

The title *The Wilde Legacy* was chosen, for both conference and book, for its emphasis on the whole Wilde family, on the multiple Irish traditions to which they had so signally contributed, on their variegated talents and on their connection to Dublin. We had intervened at an interesting moment, as a change had come over Wilde studies in the previous decade. A Trinity medical professor in the great Irish literary-medical tradition, Davis Coakley, had forcefully argued in *The Importance of being Irish* that Oscar Wilde's Irishness had been somehow wished away by the critics and that its central significance needed to be reinstated by the interpreters of his life and work. His book, and Richard Pine's which appeared just a year later, were influential; other writers have since developed the theme.[1] The close connection between Wilde and his parents and their cultural and political milieu came into focus. It thus seemed important to the planners of our celebration to look at the various strands of their activities (medical, antiquarian, political and poetic – the list is always too long for any

1 See D. Coakley, *Oscar Wilde: The Importance of being Irish* (Dublin, 1994); J. McCormack (ed.), *Wilde the Irishman* (New Haven and London, 1998); R. Pine, *The Thief of Reason: Oscar Wilde and Modern Ireland* (Dublin, 1995).

sentence it appears in) and to see those parents in their own right rather than bathed in the reflected light of a famous son. So the book of the conference opens with Lady Wilde, Speranza as she called herself and became known.

To return Wilde to Ireland had been overdue in the 1990s. In a sense he had already been returned to his family, but even the titles of the earlier biographies of the parents, T.G. Wilson's *Victorian Doctor* (1942) and Terence de Vere White's *The Parents of Oscar Wilde* (1967) with their emphasis on period and on the subordination of the parents to the son, seemed a deliberate limitation of the scope of their personalities. We can imagine many reminiscences of these extraordinary progenitors reflected in the oblique mirror of Oscar's art. But commentators have too often raised the question of his individuality only to class him as a genius whose eccentricities are forgiven because his work belongs in a detached aesthetic realm – or because he came from an eccentric family. To see this collection of kind, unconventional, fertile, talented, articulate (the list is getting too long again) Irish Victorians in terms only of period, or pathology, or canonicity, is to miss the main lesson of the resilience of the family unit in its more unexpected forms. We can see them also building disciplines (such as folklore) which had hardly existed before their time, contributing to essential bodies of knowledge about their country, influencing the development of institutions such as the Royal Irish Academy which remain vital parts of our intellectual life. To a remarkable extent, all of the three Wildes considered in this book belonged to rapidly developing tendencies in Ireland, and in the culture of the English-speaking world, which were to unfold their full meaning only after all three of them were dead.

The world they belonged to, the public world of Ireland in the nineteenth century, was deeply divided in religion, culture and politics but, in spite of – even because of – that, possessed a vitality which is perhaps only now being appreciated. Publishing, journalism, bookmaking and an appetite for work distinguished them all three. William Wilde could make a book out of a sequence of articles as cannily as any lazy hack, and then could take on a huge task of cataloguing the Academy's antiquities in the public interest. Speranza could write seditious articles, translate European mysticism, publish her husband's posthumous work and set out in her late fifties to make a literary career in London. Oscar wrote and edited journalism, lectured, signed autographs and cashed in on celebrity. She and Oscar promoted each other. But they had more than that in common. They shared with William a special awareness of the past, which spoke to them with an authority partly deriving from its aesthetic appeal, but having little to do with piety. William Wilde's despairing lament for the devastation of popular life caused by the Famine, the link with the past which has been broken, expresses a sense of the break in tradition which in its way is as radical as Speranza's revolutionary poem on the same subject. Later, Oscar and his mother's (and his wife's) fascination with costume leads to a theatricalisation of life and culture which makes possible a cultural revolution, as fashion becomes a willed revival of the past. Ancient forms of narrative, Biblical, heroic and popular, appealed to all of them; they knew the gothic impact of myth and fable and could see how narrative might remake the world, independently of its possible relationship with truth. And in spite of the deft way with nostalgia, many of the revolutions of the twentieth century, the humane as well as the brutal, are implicit in their preoccupations.

The present book, like the conference that created it, has focussed on the history of the Wildes in Dublin, on Oscar Wilde's writings for children and the theatre, and on the historic significance of his trial. These latter remain in our day of more than ordinary interest, all areas of interaction with a sometimes astonished and frequently uncivil audience. On the other hand, for Irish readers with their proverbial appetite for history, for the local and the professional, the appeal of the Dublin Victorian Wildes is still compelling. Davis Coakley, Peter Froggatt and Michael Ryan bring the grandeurs and limitations, especially of William, to new life. And it was particularly gratifying, a hundred years after Oscar Wilde's death, to be able to assemble a group of contributors for whom his writings are alive in contemporary use, in the theatre and in the context of children's reading. Robert Dunbar's essay gives us the nineteenth-century background but also juxtaposes Wildean decadence with some modern writing which is often felt to be equally subversive and unsuitable for children.

Wilde in theatre and film is still news. We were able to make this point by commissioning a play, Thomas Kilroy's *My Scandalous Life*, about Lord Alfred Douglas (a sequel to his *The Secret Fall of Constance Wilde*) which was performed at the Peacock Theatre during the conference, as well as a play for children, *The Star-Child* (adapted by Mary Elizabeth Burke-Kennedy and directed by Bairbre Ní Chaoimh with costumes by Kei Ito and settings by Chisato Yoshimi) based on the fairytales, which was produced by Storytellers Theatre in Dublin in December 2000–January 2001, and later toured Ireland in the winter of 2001–2002. Marina Carr, Michael Colgan, Thomas Kilroy, and Patrick Mason discussed the larger question of the popularity and the stature of Wilde's own plays in the new millennium, and their own direct involvement with Irish theatre enabled them to ask some irreverent questions.

Lucy McDiarmid and Alan Sinfield's essays repoliticise Oscar Wilde, McDiarmid by restoring our sense of the precise historical moment of his trial and the changes which had come about by the time he wrote *De Profundis*, Sinfield by his sweeping and swooping overview of what his name has meant in the closet/outrage politics of the twentieth century. Lucy McDiarmid has also helped us to see Wilde in a new Irish-British context, one extending from Wilfrid Scawen Blunt to Roger Casement to Brendan Behan. Alan Sinfield has incidentally completed the circle, leading us back to Davis Coakley's (and earlier Mícheál Mac Liammóir's) reclaiming of Wilde as Irish, pointing to the ways in which the question of his sexuality has been aligned with nationality.

To speak more personally, I have enjoyed editing this book; if I have a regret it is that nobody has written a piece about Oscar Wilde's criticism, since I am always astonished at how freshly it reads even as one spots the insights which have become founding tenets of so much modern writing.

My own first encounter with Oscar Wilde's writing was in a handwritten notebook of my mother's; at school in the 1930s she had copied out the whole of *The Ballad of Reading Gaol*. As most of the older generation of my family had been in gaol I found nothing surprising about this and was very willing to accept Wilde as a martyr in due course, and to see in the archaising ballad form a version of the pastiches (often Gaelicising) that were everywhere in the Irish poetry my elders fancied. (Not that the family was as liberal as all that; my grandmother recruited Guards to the cast of the plays in Taibhdhearc na Gaillimhe, when she was designing costumes there, to keep an eye on the morals of Edwards and MacLiammóir.) Later, the teenagers of my generation bought and read the one-volume

Works, which cost a pound, and taught us a great deal about life and art – though we may have learned as much from *Vera or the Nihilists* as from 'The Decay of Lying'.

My last – call it an encounter – was different. In the cemetery of Père Lachaise I went with my husband to pay my respects to Wilde, fighting my way past the fans of Jim Morrison. There was the Epstein monument with the slightly prissy inscription; and as well, not only the graffiti which appear in the 1995 photograph in the *Complete Letters*,[2] but, pushed at the side of the stone, little bunches of flowers, and *letters* – notes on small scraps of paper: 'Dear Oscar'; whispered messages of admiration and allegiance. More than any writer, he has remained present throughout the century after his death as inspiration, as accuser and as warning. The essays in this book are written by people for whom not only Oscar but Sir William Wilde and Speranza too are living, complex influences.

Eiléan Ní Chuilleanáin

2 M. Holland and R. Hart-Davis (eds), *The Complete Letters of Oscar Wilde* (London, 2000), facing p. 695.

THE WILDE FAMILY

Speranza, an ancestor for a woman poet in 2000

EILÉAN NÍ CHUILLEANÁIN

My first acquaintance with the work of Speranza was as a child in Cork reading a book of Irish fairytales from various sources. The present battered and tattered state of that book gives testimony to the diligence with which as children we read and re-read it, and one story sticks in my mind with especial tenacity, the story of the horned women. The name at the end of the last page was *Lady Wilde.*

The second time I met her was in a book, a pamphlet rather, that was battered and tattered even before I came to it. It was one of those collections called 'songbooks', actually a mixture of Irish songs and patriotic recitations, the favourite reading of servant girls in the 1940s and 50s, and there I found her poem 'The Brothers' on the trial of the brothers Sheares. It probably interested me because the Sheares brothers came from Cork, but its shadowy lamplit atmosphere stayed with me.

The name again was *Lady Wilde;* it was much later that I found out that she had called herself Speranza and read her other writings and her son's and some of her husband's. She was there, in that early cocoon of family and household and nature, her married name was inscribed on part of the wrappings of my life as a child, that life I had to emerge from before I could become a writer. Later, when I stood at a little distance from that life – and surely reading Oscar Wilde and, as a teenager, reading about him, was one of the ways that we had, in the mid-twentieth century, of learning about the powerful, dangerous winds you let into your life when you step out of childhood – when I was thinking of myself as a writer, I saw how much in his mother's poetry and the poetry of many of her female successors simply wouldn't do, then, as a model.

I'm glad now to return to her again, to look at the gulf that lay between us at that time, and to ask how real it was, whether it could ever be bridged. And beyond that, what use our female predecessors are to us as women writers, what is the function of model, teacher, exemplar?

It's easy to celebrate Speranza, there's so much about her that appeals to our age and her own. Her courage, her tolerance, her kindness are vividly attested – the stories are all memorable, whether or not it's absolutely true that she stood up in the gallery at the trial of Gavan Duffy and shouted, 'I wrote that article' or alternatively articulated in a low musical voice, 'I am the culprit, if culprit there be.' Or that she allowed a lover of her husband's to sit in the room with him day after day as he lay dying, or that when after his death there was no money and the bailiffs were in the house she sat in her Merrion Square drawing-room unconcerned, reading *Prometheus Bound* aloud to herself in Greek.[1]

The tellers of the stories are sometimes prejudiced, sometimes unsympathetic, sometimes inclined to make her a figure of fun. This continues long after her death; twentieth-century knowingness adds sexual innuendo. Terence de Vere White in his life of Sir William and herself had to suggest that she was undersexed – the worst possible allegation in the 1960s. Even without the anecdotes there is plenty of evidence that she was public-spirited, talented, learned, very loyal to her family and very kind to the young.[2]

In considering her as a writer and an ancestor-figure to other writers I want first of all to take account of that person, to say that it matters to me that she had these virtues, as well as others which are more particularly relevant to the profession of writing. And not just to me. The personal virtues one might have as a woman or simply as a human being keep coming into discussions of Irish women as writers – at times, over the last hundred and fifty years, into discussions of whether one should be allowed to be a professional writer at all. There's a story from ten years ago of a woman who declared that she couldn't let her neighbours know she wrote poetry because 'They'd think it meant that I didn't wash my windows.' In the mid-1950s my own mother was visited by a solemn embassy from her family to tell her that she ought to give up writing and publishing. These concerned relatives declared that they thought she must be neglecting her

1 J. Melville, *Mother of Oscar* (London, 1994), pp 39, 128–9, 142.   2 See T. de Vere White, *The Parents of Oscar Wilde, Sir William and Lady Wilde* (London, 1967), pp 126–7, 229, 258.

house and her children. They changed their mind when she told them what she earned (and the reality of earning for the woman writer has always mattered far beyond its cash value). The fact that she wrote when we were at school and that she spent her earnings on taking us on holidays didn't excuse *her* – but the money showed that the writing somehow worked. It stopped her being an embarrassment. That was the important thing: not to embarrass one's family. William, Speranza and Oscar Wilde all did, and the other son Willie, with his marital adventures, tried hard to keep up.

But my mother wrote prose fiction. In the twentieth century, poetry has been an embarrassment because in almost all cases it does not pay. There has been no economic excuse for it, and thus it has represented feelings gratuitously expressed, and made readers feel uneasy about what revelations might be about to burst out, made them feel that poets belong with the safely dead. And there used to be an assumption that one wrote about one's own life. Perhaps it is that assumption, applied in a special way to women writers, that has caused many of us to become so oblique and contorted in our writing. A refusal to write autobiography in my own case has in the end brought me closer to some of Speranza's writing, as I hope to show.

We see her in the frame of the Victorian age and it's a relief to see her as anything but an angel in the house. She had the virtues of a woman writer and they made her an embarrassment to some. These virtues include her reputation as a lousy housekeeper, her habit of getting up late – ten or eleven in a morning – and only writing in her dressing-gown,[3] her focus on getting published, the mark of a true hack or professional if you will. And with that goes her determination to hit a public voice and the sheer vigour of her self-invention, achieved with the enthusiastic collaboration of her audience in Ireland and Irish-America.[4]

It was not normal for a woman to have a public – and she didn't want to be normal. When she was making a living in London writing for magazines she observed that:

3 Melville, pp 46–7.   4 See Melville, p. 167, for the applause which greeted Oscar Wilde's mention of his mother's connection with *The Nation* in San Francisco; also M. Howes, 'Tears and Blood: Lady Wilde and the Emergence of Irish Cultural Nationalism' in T. Foley and S. Ryder (eds), *Ideology and Ireland in the Nineteenth Century* (Dublin, 1998), pp 151–72, at pp 152–3 .

> It has been computed that about 16,000 women in London live by literature, that is, that there are amongst us 16,000 bundles of abnormal nerves and sensibilities and quivering emotions, fiery fancies, tumultuous passions and throbbing brains, all working day and night to formulate themselves into words.[5]

She has the necessary egotism of the writer; 'mais je suis vraiment egoiste', she says in a letter. A relieved uncle – relieved at getting her off his hands when she married Wilde – observed that 'the love of self is the prominent feature of her character.'[6] The writer's egotism, often expressing itself in eccentricity, makes the writing and especially the continuing to write possible. Eccentricity is a giving hostages to fortune, a willingness to look ridiculous if one fails, knowing that one will not be forgiven for failure. A willingness to embarrass. But if we are to consider the importance of her example for women writers of a later generation, it's partly in that lesson, that it is possible to have a warm and generous character and to look after and remain close to one's children while holding on to the egotism that makes one a writer. It's both as a person and as the kind of writer she is that she functions as exemplar and ancestor.

We might as well say now that the kind of poet she is is not the kind that as readers, more than a hundred years later, we value most. She's no Emily Dickinson or Christina Rossetti; her poetry is less attractive than say George Eliot's. She does not like Rossetti and Dickinson have something utterly personal to say, born out of a deep contemplation of their own position as women in their century. She doesn't have the quiet fidelity of George Eliot that makes Eliot's poetry so like her prose. Her chosen field is political poetry and in it she turns her eye to the immediate political effect. And this draws attention to a problem we still haven't solved at the turn of the new millennium: how poetry in our day may be effective as political persuasion and remain credible as poetry, as was possible in the era of Dryden or of Shelley.

Within the Irish political canon of her century she is a match perhaps for Thomas Davis but not for Allingham or Ferguson, certainly not for Mangan. She doesn't have the subtle echo, that sense of someone dancing

---

5 J. Wilde, *Social Studies* (London, 1893), p. 110.   6 Melville, pp 41, 51.

---

in the heavy chains of the past and the other language, the oceanic heave that we hear in Mangan. Her language and her metre are quite different. They are energetic – the ball rebounds from the back of the ball-alley so fast that we can hardly keep our eye on it. Now, to write poetry with dash like this doesn't work, since in most cases the reader of poetry wants to think a bit. Speranza needs something to slow her down, and in fact the most successful of her poems with their long lines and strong pauses have a drag on them, a drag of feeling as much as metre in 'The Famine Year' and in the poem on Henry and John Sheares.

Some of the extra weight that ballasts those two poems comes from their sense of real history. The historical and scholarly activity of the 1830s and 40s, from Hardiman's printing and translating of Gaelic lyrics in 1831 to O'Donovan's edition of the *Annals of the Four Masters* in 1848–51, lies behind so much of the later poetry of the Irish nineteenth century. In this context it is interesting that, for Speranza, it is the history of the present that matters most, and when she turns to the past, it's the most recent past. Dr R.R. Madden's *History of the United Irishmen* of 1842 supplies the account of the Sheares trial from 1798.[7] She follows Madden quite faithfully; he has the darkness illuminated by oil-lamps because it was after midnight when the jury retired; he has the details about the judge's apparent sympathy with the families of the two men, the speech of Henry Sheares interrupted by tears:

> 'Tis midnight, falls the lamplight dull and sickly
> On a pale and anxious crowd,
> Through the court, and round the judges, thronging thickly,
> With prayers none dare to speak aloud ...
> Twice the judge essayed to speak the word – to-morrow –
> Twice faltered, as a woman he had been.
> To-morrow! – Fain the elder would have spoken,
> Prayed for respite, tho' it is not Death he fears;
> But, thoughts of home and wife his heart hath broken,
> And his words are stopped by tears ...[8]

7 R.R. Madden, *The United Irishmen, their Lives and Times* (London, 1842), ii, pp 174–95.   8 J. Wilde, *Poems by Speranza* (Dublin, 1864), pp 1, 3. See, on this poem and on the issues of

However, while Madden's focus is on the miscarriage of justice by which Henry Sheares was held responsible for his younger brother's actions, hers is on the inspiration for new revolutionaries to be drawn from the memory of their martyrdom. For the most part, when she wrote for *The Nation* her eye was on the present, the moment when the die is rolling; no surprise that in 1848 she wrote a poem called 'The Year of Revolutions' and that the notorious article for which Duffy was tried as editor was called *Jacta Alea Est*. She presents a striking example of what David Lloyd spoke of when he said that for the writers of *The Nation* the future mattered more than the past, that 'Total immersion of the writer's identity in the nation was seen as the first condition of a process that sought to fabricate a foreshortened literary history in which the development that had hitherto been thwarted might be speedily made up'.[9] For the scholars of her generation the fascinations of history and scholarship remained a link to the past, but Speranza as her name warns us is focused on the coming time.

Visions of the future lead her to cast herself in the role of prophet, and much of her imagery and vocabulary are religious in no loose sense of the word. But this as she realizes has its limitations. In the 'Dedication' poem addressed 'To Ireland', which appears in the second and later editions of *Poems by Speranza,* she invokes the figure of Miriam from the Book of Exodus, singing in triumph when Pharaoh's army comes to grief:

> And Miriam the prophetess, the sister of Aaron, took a timbrel in her hand; and all the women went out after her with timbrels and with dances. And Miriam answered them, Sing ye to the Lord, for he hath triumphed gloriously; the horse and the rider hath he thrown into the sea (*Exodus* 15, 20–21).

Miriam had been appealed to for centuries as a forerunner for women preachers and women poets. But for Speranza as Irish Victorian woman there can't be quite such an identification with a glorious military triumph:

gender it raises, Howes, art. cit.; see also J. Cannavan, 'Romantic Revolutionary Irishwomen: Women, Young Ireland and 1848' in M. Kelleher and J.H. Murphy (eds), *Gender perspectives in nineteenth-century Ireland: public and private spheres* (Dublin, 1997), pp 212–20. 9 D. Lloyd, *Nationalism and minor literature: James Clarence Mangan and the emergence of Irish cultural nationalism* (Berkeley and London, 1987), p. 76.

> She flung her triumphs to the stars
> In glorious chants for freedom won
> While over Pharaoh's gilded cars
> The fierce, death-bearing waves rolled on,
> I can but look in God's great face
> And pray him for our fated race ...

She is both embracing the prophetic role and confessing that it doesn't fit her in a world where women can only quietly offer inspiration.

> The woman's voice dies in the strife
> Of Liberty's awakening life ...

They have been relegated to functions connected with nursing the sick and gently inculcating Christianity.

> I only lift the funeral pall
> That so God's light might touch thine eyes
> And ring the silver prayer-bell clear
> To rouse thee from thy trance of fear ...[10]

(Is the bell, as in Thomas Moore's song, related to the bell of St Patrick that disenchanted the Children of Lir?)

Political prophecy was alive and well in early nineteenth-century Ireland, among the Gaelic-speaking people.[11] The literati of the *Nation* too are interested in the poetic visions of the eighteenth century, the *Aisling* in which the poet encounters a female figure, first grieving for Ireland's wrongs and then proclaiming the imminent salvation of the country through the restoration of the Stuarts. To speak as a prophetic woman may then be to take the place of the female figure of the *Aisling*. In

10 J. Wilde, *Poems by Speranza* (Glasgow, 1867), pp iii-iv. 11 See the references, for example in Máire Bhuí Ní Laoghaire's 'Cath Chéim an Fhia' (1822), to the apocalyptic work by 'Pastorini' – actually the pseudonym of an English bishop, Charles Walmesley – *General History of the Christian Church, from her birth, to her final triumphant state in heaven, chiefly deduced from the Apocalypse of St John the Apostle* (n.p., 1771), which foretold the downfall of Protestantism. See *Filíocht Mháire Bhuidhe Ní Laoghaire*, Donncha Ó Donnchú do chnuasaigh (Baile Átha Cliath, 1933).

Speranza's 'The Famine Year' however, she assumes the role of the usually male poet, of the interrogator, the one to whom the dreadful vision has to be explained:

> Weary men what reap ye? Golden corn for the stranger.
> What sow ye? Human corpses that wait for the avenger.

The men in this poem deny their manhood; they reap and sow like automata but in their personal lives they are bankrupt:

> No; the blood is dead within our veins – we care not now for life;
> Let us die hid in the ditches, far from children and from wife;
> We cannot stay and listen to their raving, famished cries ...[12]

Like the lady of the *Aisling* they can only mourn and hope for a saviour. The parallel may gain some force from the fact that the major poet of the *Nation* had translated several of the originals of the genre; James Clarence Mangan's *The Poets and Poetry of Munster*, posthumously published in 1849, included at least six poems in the *Aisling* convention.[13]

Mangan revels in the visionary and archaic quality of the Gaelic tradition; by contrast, the strongest influence on most of Speranza's poetry is biblical, the imagery of a Messiah that fits with her revolutionary temper and perhaps also her Protestant and partly clerical background. But if her prophetic voice is markedly less despairing in many of her poems than in the gloom of 'The Famine Year', the poems often express the limitations of the woman's role rather than envisioning any potential for women's action. Or they express, as in 'The Exodus', frustration and blame at the inaction of Ireland's governors faced with the depopulation due to famine and emigration, which her husband's work had statistically documented. The tone remains apocalyptic:

> Ye stand at the Judgement-bar today –
> The Angels are counting the dead-roll, too;

---

12 *Poems by Speranza*, 1864, pp 5–6.   13 See J. Chuto et al. (eds), *The collected works of James Clarence Mangan* (Dublin, 1996–99), vol. iv, pp 143, 148–9, 161, 167–9, 203–4, 205–7.

Have ye trod in the pure and perfect way,
  And ruled for God as the crowned should do?
Count our dead – before angels and men
Ye're judged and doomed by the Statist's pen.[14]

The prophetic strain is involved at some point with the formation of an Irish canon. When Yeats writes 'to Ireland in the coming times'[15] he is addressing, rather than a literary posterity, a political unit that does not yet exist but which will have its own canon in which he aligns himself with the poets of the *Nation*. Is it plausible for a woman poet at the turn of the twenty-first century to look back and claim a similar succession? What considerations, of public and private voice, of canonicity, of continuity, are implied?

To start with the issue of continuity: considering the line of male poets from Mangan to Ferguson to Yeats, and the lively succession wars of the twentieth century, a woman has to face a contrasting break in the female tradition which may lead one to believe it either does not exist or will have to be reinvented. There is a succession that goes from Speranza to Katharine Tynan, – she knew, and was good to, Tynan in London and it was Tynan who introduced her to the young Yeats. This, though, is a line of poets who have some political interests but who are becoming more domestic all the time. Compare Speranza's light-hearted exclamation on caring for her first baby: 'Gruel and the nursery cannot end me',[16] with the weighty sense of total responsibility in Katharine Tynan's 'Any Woman':

I am the pillars of the house
The keystone of the arch am I
Take me away, and roof and wall
Would fall to ruin utterly
I am the fire upon the hearth,
I am the light of the good sun,
I am the heat which warms the earth,
Which else were colder than a stone.

---

14 *Poems by Speranza*, 1864, pp 55–7.   15 W.B. Yeats, *Collected Poems* (London, 1955), p. 56.
16 Melville, p. 57.

> ... I am the house from floor to roof,
> I deck the walls, the board I spread;
> I spin the curtains, warp and woof,
> And shake the down to be their bed.
>
> I am their wall against all danger,
> Their door against the wind and snow.
> Thou whom a woman laid in manger,
> Take me not till the children grow![17]

The grammatical impossibility of the first line suggests the hysteria of one who is embracing an impossible task. We do hear Speranza's prophetic voice again in Eva Gore-Booth, especially in the volume of 1906, *The Egyptian Pillar*. Poems like 'Comrades', 'Women's Rights', 'The Street Orator' and 'On the Embankment' reflect Gore-Booth's life as an agitator. In 'Women's Trades on the Embankment' the sentiment is a fury of exasperation. The Prime Minister had told the Women's Franchise deputation of 1906 to 'have patience' – that quintessentially feminine virtue. She welds together impatience at his patronizing response with (I think, given the emphasis of the title) anger at the degradation of prostitutes. Her voice is Biblical, in fact almost Blakean as the Thames Embankment becomes the shore of the Red Sea:

> Where the Egyptian pillar – old, so old –
> With mystery fronts the open English sky,
> Bearing the yoke of those who heap up gold,
> The sad-eyed workers pass in silence by ...
>
> Long has submission played a traitor's part –
> Oh human soul, no patience anymore
> Shall break your wings and harden Pharaoh's heart,
> And keep you lingering on the Red Sea shore.[18]

And then there's a silence. There are plenty of women writing in the period before 1922, followed by an absence of women who are any kind of

17 K. Tynan, *Poems*, ed. M. Gibbon (Dublin, 1963), pp 24–5.   18 E. Gore-Booth, *Poems* (London, 1929), pp 404–5.

serious contenders. The first new woman poet to make a mark is Máire Mhac an tSaoi in *Margadh na Saoire* in the 1950s.[19] She constructs an ancestry for herself by appealing to a Gaelic tradition, by writing in Irish, and by identification with a semi-legendary figure, Máire Ní Ógáin. Was it, or is it, possible for English-language women poets to construct a similar ancestry which would include Speranza?

Perhaps I should say how that question affects me. I'm by a year or so the oldest of a generation of women poets who began to write and publish from the 1960s on. I say 'generation'; there were poets before us, Eithne Strong, who died in 1999, and Leland Bardwell, fortunately still publishing. And there was, particularly for me and for others with access to the language, the example of Máire Mhac an tSaoi. But as a teenager I had no awareness of living women poets in English, while in my time, say since 1964 when I was first published in a newspaper, there has been a reasonably high profile for women as poets, one that contrasts with the experience from the 1920s on. In that interval, there had been no shortage of women prose writers both Irish and foreign, both past and present, carrying on a succession that ran from Maria Edgeworth and Jane Austen to Kate O'Brien and Virginia Woolf, to Iris Murdoch and Edna O'Brien. Women writing for children and adults, in popular and elite genres, in England and Ireland. But in England and Ireland women had been, as it were, warned off writing poetry – as if indeed the pansified reputation of the poet after Oscar Wilde had made it emphatically necessary to make poetry safe for males by insisting on its macho credentials – and to challenge that exclusion seemed worth doing.

What made it possible to start? In my own case, vanity, and the presence of a professional woman writer in my family. To be female writing poetry suggested itself to me as exciting, because I felt women's experience had changed since Katharine Tynan's day, one would be exploring and expressing, it seemed, a whole world that had not been experienced by Irish women before. I said so to a male poet who replied that he saw women's experiences as invariably more predictable than men's. And, like him, many readers expected a female writer of poetry to choose domestic subjects – when I was twenty-three, for Heaven's sake, discovering the lit-

---

19 M. Mhac an tSaoi, *Margadh na saoire: bailiúchán véarsaí* (Baile Átha Cliath, 1956).

erary pubs of Dublin, with an academic salary, no responsibilities and even a car of my own. The mismatch between the accepted view of women's lives as subject matter and the actuality of women's literary projects continued up into the 1970s. My own neglect of overtly personal and domestic themes led to me being described as a female impersonator rather than a woman poet.

The mismatch between individual motives and the public's expectations may not have existed in the same way in the nineteenth century. There may have been no suppressed sense that there was an undiscovered subject-matter for poetry, women's own view of their lives. The fact that much poetry by women on political as well as personal themes was published in periodicals aimed at a general readership suggests a consensus which was far from ruling out a woman having a role as a writer. The literary and journalistic activity of women in Speranza's day flourished and is well documented. But the restriction of poetry to a minority readership in the twentieth century entails a breakdown of consensus, and has thus created a double break in the female line: in women's relationship with the past, and with the general audience for literature.

Well, what has changed in my time? The audience has, for a start. We don't know what size the audience for Irish poetry was in the nineteenth century. We don't know if there was a *feminine* audience for poetry by women. There may have been. In the mid-twentieth century there was a tiny audience. There had until recently been almost no Irish publishing.

Ireland changed. There were great demographic, legal and economic changes, all affecting women, and there were political issues seen as especially theirs like divorce, contraception ... By the 1970s there was beginning to be an audience for poetry that expected women poets to say something that was particularly about their experiences. One couldn't always oblige. Was this a reversion to something parallel to the situation in previous passages in the country's history, in the 1840s when Speranza wrote and poetry was part of the Young Ireland programme, or in the 1890s, when Yeats encountered enthusiastic, demanding audiences, whose expectations and motives he knew were not his?[20] I can't tell.

But I do know too that the new audience with its own agenda was outside the critical establishment. Some things did not change. When I start-

20 W.B. Yeats, *Autobiographies* (London, 1955), pp 200–5.

ed to write I had a good idea of what that establishment would and would not tolerate. One would not be allowed to be *strident,* that is to assert one's female presence, though one might allow it to be gathered or guessed. Feminism was embarrassing. The past was embarrassing. Speranza with her salons, Isadora Duncan with her draperies, Oscar with his precious poetry and his passion were embarrassing though his wit was all right.

Irony and detachment were what was needed, we were to search for objective correlatives and avoid the vulgarly kinetic. And by and large that's where we still are in terms of mainstream critical expectations. The boundaries have been tested but they are still there. The distinction, still there as it was in 1970, between poetry that tells it straight and poetry that uses artful strategies, has a particular application to women poets.

And as we couldn't be Stephen Dedalus and we didn't all want to be Molly Bloom, some of us had to devise our own strategies to write our poems as women. There are women poets who are really continuing the Katharine Tynan tradition into an Ireland where domestic and sexual issues have become public issues. I've read recently that many Irish women poets 'don't give a toss for the idea of the nation. Their concerns are more quotidian, their poems born out of unvarnished daily living.'[21] Doesn't that sound worthy? To me it sounds like a recipe for dullness, since it's especially the varnish, or perhaps the high polish of Victorian furniture *and what it reflects*, that attracts the onlooker and at last sets us afloat on that sea of conflicting meanings.

We *could* ignore all that history and assume that we have to make everything starting from scratch. We *could* abjure artfulness and strategy and obliquity and contemplate our daily tasks; we could make this a theory of women's poetry. But this leaves women it seems to me as the new peasantry, deprived of history and entrapped in immemorial labours. And the problem is that *it isn't true* that we, as Irish women writers in English, are merely creatures of the present and the few poor shreds of family reminiscence that we can pull around ourselves. We do have female ancestors in the nineteenth century, as research is amply demonstrating.[22] We may be at odds with these ancestors, as with the history of our own time, but

21 P. O'Brien, 'Introduction' in P. O'Brien (ed.), *The Wake Forest Book of Irish Women's Poetry 1967–2000* (Winston-Salem, N.C., 1999), p. xxv. **22** For example by the work of the Munster Women Writers' Project at University College, Cork.

wé are not 'outside history' in any sense but that of a willful metaphor. The writers, scholars and translators of the past do not always provide us with, in any simple sense, inspiring exemplars, but their existence is part of our reality.

So I'd like to conclude by looking at the possibilities for us now, of looking back into that phantasmagoria of reflections that is the past, and the ways in which we may be indebted to Speranza in our strategic devisings. Especially in her role of folklorist; since this is a way – along with literary and linguistic and historical scholarship – of contacting the feminine past and identifying ourselves in ways that leave us free to use irony, playfulness and fantasy. It is by way of the insidious pleasures of folklore that more than one woman poet has found her way to expressing her passions and her ideas, and that I find myself encountering Speranza and the ambiguous fragments she published again.

The use of themes from folklore and folktale is not a simple solution for the woman poet's problems of identification. Many of the poets of the Revival used such themes and it's a sobering sight now to see how stiff and how shallow some of their work sounds. I can find a reason for this in a manner that stresses the voice's naivety – as in Nora Hopper Chesson's 'The Short Cut to the Rosses' for example[23] – and thus exhibits the peasant speaker as curiosity. On the other hand, consider Yeats's 'Song of Wandering Aengus' – what makes that such a stunning poem still? I think it's partly the contrast between the demented old man, occupying a role recognised by peasant society, and the glorious vision of youth; and partly the fact that the speaker admits desire: he goes out to the hazel-wood 'because a fire was in my head', and the unexplained actions and unexpected developments all follow from the reality of that desire that does not know an object and then finds one. For so many of the poets in Eilís Ní Dhuibhne's splendid anthology, *Voices on the Wind*, the object is only too recognisable from the start: it is love as a conventional theme with nothing surprising about it. In Dora Sigerson Shorter's 'All Soul's Night' there *is* a surprising sentiment, a clash between the individual's experience and the tradition. The girl goes through all the steps to conjure up the ghost of her lover:

23 In E. Ní Dhuibhne (ed.), *Voices on the Wind: Women Poets of the Celtic Twilight* (Dublin, 1995), p. 140.

O mother, mother, I swept the hearth, I set his chair and the white
board spread,
I prayed for his coming to our kind Lady when Death's sad doors
would let out the dead;
A strange wind rattled the window-pane, and down the lane a dog
howled on …

– but when he comes she is terrified:

My woe forever, that I could not sever coward flesh from fear;
His chair put aside when the young cock cried, and I was afraid to
meet my dear.[24]

There has to be some gritty sense for us to take hold of, a sense of the real
thing, or what we experience as reality because it surprises us – as in Nuala
Ní Dhomhnaill's poetry, where 'Bean an Leasa' (the fairy woman) comes
armed with a Black and Decker to cut down trees in the speaker's subur-
ban garden, or in 'Bean an Leasa mar Shíobshiúlóir' appears as a
hitch-hiker who seduces with gifts of videotapes, cameras and computers,
or in 'An Bhatráil' where the theme of the child stolen by the fairies
merges disturbingly with the battered baby syndrome.[25] Folklore does not
belong only in a fading past or with a heavily symbolic peasant culture.

To return to my first encounter with Speranza: her folkloric writings
stress not naivety but the depth and variety of Irish tradition. The power
of 'The Horned Women'[26] is in part in its exciting compression, and the
way details appear when they are needed. It starts with an image of power
and security, 'A rich woman sat up late one night carding and preparing
wool, while all the family and servants were asleep.' The woman's house is
invaded by twelve witches who sit carding and spinning wool and terrify
their hostess. They order her to fetch water from the well. A benevolent

24 D. Sigerson Shorter, *Collected Poems* (London, 1907), p. 119.   **25** N. Ní Dhomhnaill,
Pharaoh's Daughter (Loughcrew, Co. Meath, 1990), pp 36–8; (with translations into English
by M. McGuckian and E. Ní Chuilleanáin) *The Water Horse* (Loughcrew, 1992), pp 10–11;
(with translations into English by P. Muldoon) *The Astrakhan Cloak* (Loughcrew, 1992), pp
24–5.   **26** J. Wilde, *Ancient Legends, Mystic Charms, and Superstitions of Ireland. With
Sketches of the Irish Past* (Galway, 1971), pp 10–12.

spirit speaks from the well and tells her how to trick them into leaving, and how to lay spells around the house by the time they come back, to deny them entry, and so she does:

> she sprinkled the water in which she had washed her child's feet (the feet-water) outside the door on the threshold … she took the cake which the witches had made during her absence of meal mixed with the blood drawn from the sleeping family. And she broke the cake in bits, and placed a bit in the mouth of each sleeper, and they were restored; and she took the cloth they had woven and placed it half in and half out of the chest with the padlock …

We only learn of the child and the danger it runs two-thirds of the way through the story, and that danger is both extreme – threatening a life-essence contained in the water and blood – and unexplained. Shortly after, there is a reference to 'children' in the plural; the central figure's task becomes heavier, as in a nightmare. But as the tension grows the reader's experience is also pleasurable in a different way; the spells play with the thresholds and locks of the house, and with bodily thresholds, the bodies of the sleepers, and the effect is mysteriously satisfying, as I felt when I read the story as a child:

> 'Open! open!' they screamed. 'Open, feet-water!'
> 'I cannot,' said the feet-water, 'I am scattered on the ground and my path is down to the Lough.'
> … 'Open, open, cake that we have made and mingled with blood,' they cried again.
> 'I cannot,' said the cake, 'for I am broken and bruised, and my blood is on the lips of the sleeping children.'

I have never lost the frisson that those words produced the first time that I read them. The story seems all the more remarkable with hindsight. It is not at all surprising that the twenty-three year old Yeats placed it first in his collection, *Fairy and Folk Tales of the Irish Peasantry* in 1888. It has the compelling ironies and narrative peripeteia of his own poems and tales on folk themes; it makes a claim like them to heroic stature.

While the folktale was widely disseminated in Ireland in Speranza's life-
time, and has been found in many places in the twentieth century as well,
there is something special about her retelling of it. Versions from Kilkenny
and Wexford had been collected before hers appeared, suggesting that the
Wexford background of her childhood may be relevant. These other versions can be wordy and given to over-explanation; for example, in the story
as told in a manuscript preserved in the Prim papers, when the woman goes
to the well, '... a man appeared before her (either a friendly ghost, or a
human friend in the fairies) and with evident concern appeased her fears
and agitation. 'Unhappy woman' said he, 'the strange intruders who have
sent you hither are fairies whose displeasure you have incurred.'[27] Oral versions can suggest a moralistic reading. In the version collected from Cáit
('An Bhab') Feirtéar of Dunquin, on which Eilís Ní Dhuibhne based her
marvellous play, *Dún na mBan Trí Thine,* the spirit who speaks from the
well is the woman's mother. She tells her to wash mugs, plates and other
household objects and put them in their correct places – the mugs and
plates in the dresser, the tongs standing in the fireplace. One moral may be
the need to keep an orderly home. The Dunquin storyteller also emphasis-
es the fact that the woman is alone in the house, her husband and son having gone to the mainland from the Blasket island where this version is set
– thus another lesson may be the necessary dependance of women on their
menfolk for security. Áine O'Neill also comments that 'In many variants of
the story, we are also given the message that one should not stay up working late at night ... The recurring themes of warnings against sloth,
uncleanliness and untidiness are of significance in the cultural as well as the
educational context.' By contrast, Speranza's version defies the expectations
of moral-hunting readers and thus becomes fully a text of its time.

Finally, it has a political as well as an aesthetic meaning. The narrative
motif appears not to be found outside Ireland, and to be connected with
the Sliabh na mBan area in South Tipperary.[28] With its topographical and
national authenticity it can be said to earn its pride of position in
Speranza's *Ancient Legends.* She introduces it as 'weird and strange, ... [a]
mythical story, translated from the Irish, and which is said to be a thou-

27 Á. O'Neill, '"The Fairy Hill is on Fire" (MLSIT 6071): A panorama of multiple functions',
in *Béaloideas* 59 (1991), 189–96, at p. 191.   28 Art. cit., pp 194, 192.

33

sand years old'[29]; and in fact it shows a kinship with ancient tales of visitations by ferocious female other-world figures from the Morrigu to the Banshee.[30] The placing and introducing of the story make it part of a claim for the separateness, antiquity and cultural value of the Irish imagination, and thus, obliquely, it serves Speranza's political ends. I hope we can continue to learn from her wiliness.

29 *Ancient Legends*, p. 10. 30 See P. Lysaght, *The Banshee: The Irish Supernatural Death-messenger* (Dun Laoghaire, 1986).

Oscar Wilde and the
Wildes of Merrion Square

DAVIS COAKLEY

On 12 November 1851, at a quiet wedding in Dublin, the eye and ear surgeon William Wilde married the poet Jane Francesca Elgee. Their first child
was born eleven months later. He was given the names William Charles
Kingsbury, names drawn from those of his father, his maternal grandfather
and grandmother. The second child was born on 16 October 1854, and was
given the names Oscar Fingal O'Fflahertie, names from Irish history and
mythology.[1] Oscar Wilde grew up in a remarkable medical and cultural
milieu which was centred on Merrion Square in the middle of the nineteenth century. It was a time when Dublin had a leading international
school of medicine largely due to the efforts of an outstanding group of
physicians and surgeons. Many of these men, one of whom was Oscar's
father, William Wilde, lived near each other in Merrion Square and they
were known not only for their medical reputations but also for their interest in the arts and literature.[2] They attracted the leaders of the cultural life
of Dublin to their tables and, in the words of Oliver St John Gogarty, at
these dinners 'wit and anecdote circulated with the port'.[3]

Oscar's mother, Jane Elgee, although descended from a distinguished
Anglo-Irish family, abandoned the political values of her family when she

1 ff was used in old manuscripts for F. This led to a fashion for adopting ff in certain surnames
beginning with F. The ff spelling was adopted by the leading Galway Norman families such as
ffrench and ffont. As the Celtic O'Flaherty clan began to submit to English rule in the sixteenth
and seventeenth centuries in order to protect their land, some branches began to adopt the ff
spelling probably as a signal of their loyalty and nobility. Some confused the situation by using Ff
instead of ff (see *Oxford English Dictionary*). This happened when Oscar Wilde's name was
entered in the baptismal register of St Mark's Church where his name appears as Oscar Fingal
O'Fflahertie Wilde. Fingal is the Gaelic for fair-haired stranger. It was used by the Scotsman James
McPherson in *Ossian* as the name of Fionn, leader of the Fianna, father of Oisín and grandfather
of Oscar. The name Wills is not among his registered baptismal names but was added later by his
parents.   2 D. Coakley, *The Irish School of Medicine* (Dublin, 1988).   3 O. Gogarty, *Intimations*
(London, 1985), p. 31.

was a young woman and became a regular contributor to the Young Ireland publication *The Nation* under the pseudonym Speranza. An active supporter of the Young Ireland rebellion of 1848, she wrote a highly charged article for *The Nation* calling the Irish people to arms. Most of the leaders of the Young Ireland Movement were arrested and deported; Jane Elgee, however, did not face the rigours of the law. The Irish people perceived her as a national heroine, and as Oscar later recalled, she encouraged her children to 'reverence and love' the leaders and poets of Young Ireland. He listened with great interest to her stories about men such as Thomas Davis, Charles Gavan Duffy, Denis Florence MacCarthy and James Clarence Mangan. Oscar also met many of the '48 poets and grew to admire them because (as he later said) they were men 'who made their lives *noble poems also*, men who had not merely written about the sword but were able to bear it, who not only could rhyme to Liberty, but could die for her also, if need had so been'.[4] He was to have a lifelong fascination with the Young Ireland poet James Clarence Mangan (1803–49) whom he never met.

Mangan was a tragic figure whose life was ruined by opium and alcohol. Known for his beautiful translations of Irish work into English, he was a regular contributor to *The Nation*; he is probably best remembered today for his poem 'Dark Rosaleen'. Wilde thought highly of Mangan's poetry but he was also intrigued by his strange life: 'But of all the remarkable literary figures of this time none was so wonderful a genius as Clarence Mangan – the Edgar Allan Poe of our country, whose romantic life and wretched death are among the many tragedies of literature.'[5]

In his time Mangan was well known in Dublin because of his eccentric dress. He wore a steeple-shaped hat and a short blue cloak and he never went anywhere even in the finest weather without a large umbrella. According to one of his biographers, Mangan was fully aware of the strangeness of his attire: 'His scarecrow attire was as much a badge as the flaming tie of the poetaster.'[6]

Mangan wrote an essay on 'Mannerisms' in which he emphasized the importance of a pose or affectation for the man of genius: 'You shall tramp the earth in vain for a more pitiable object than a man of genius

4 H.M. Hyde, *Oscar Wilde Plays, Prose and Poems* (London, 1982), pp 373–8. 5 ibid. 6 J.B. Sheridan, *James Clarence Mangan* (Dublin, 1937), pp 57–8.

with nothing else to back it up. Transfuse into this man a due portion of mannerisms – the metamorphosis is marvellous. Senates listen, empires tremble, thrones tumble down before him.'[7] 'He has faults,' declared a writer in *The Nation* on Mangan's death in 1849 'but the inexpiable sin of commonplace no man can lay to his charge'.[8] The same could later be said of Oscar Wilde.

From the early years of their marriage, William and Jane Wilde gathered around them the leading writers, artists and scientists of the Ireland of their day. Their homes in Dublin, first at 21 Westland Row and later at 1 Merrion Square, were known as centres of culture and of hospitality. The former was a medium-sized Georgian residence which overlooked the park of Trinity College at the rear. Among the visitors to 21 Westland Row were the artists John Hogan and George Petrie, the poet Samuel Ferguson and the scientist William Rowan Hamilton.[9] Hamilton was so brilliant as a student that he was appointed professor of Astronomy and Astronomer Royal in 1827 before he had taken his primary degree. He was one of the most outstanding mathematicians of the nineteenth century, and the Hamiltonian function is central to modern theoretical and quantum physics. Hamilton first met Speranza in April 1855 and he thought that she was 'amusingly fearless and original'.[10] At the time Speranza was arranging Oscar's baptism and she asked Hamilton to be the godfather.

> Perhaps because I was so to a grandson of Wordsworth … and because she is an admirer of Wordsworth. However, I declined. But it seems I have not fallen entirely out of favour thereby, for she paid me, on Saturday last, a visit of three hours and a half … [She] told me, as we drank a glass of wine to the health of her child, that he had been christened on the previous day, by a long baptismal name, or string of names, the two first of which are Oscar and Fingal! … She is quite a genius, and thoroughly aware of it.[11]

Hamilton began to call regularly on the Wilde's and on one occasion he brought with him a volume of poetry which had been written by his sis-

7 Ibid. 8 R. O'Fracháin, 'James Clarence Mangan' in N.J. MacManus (ed.), *Thomas Davis and Young Ireland* (Dublin, 1945), pp 61–7. 9 D. Coakley, *Oscar Wilde: The Importance of Being Irish* (Dublin, 1994), p. 30. 10 Hamilton Letters, National Library of Ireland, Ms. 905. 11 Ibid.

ter. He recalled how he walked slowly to Westland Row 'cutting the pages as I went along of the copy of my sister's volume – which operation I had time to finish before I reached the house of Dr. Wilde. I was shewn up to the Drawing-Room and Mrs Wilde soon came downstairs to see me'.[12] The Wildes were pleased that their home was becoming a meeting place for the cultural life of the city but they knew that they needed a more prestigious address, so when Oscar was still an infant the family moved from 21 Westland Row to 1 Merrion Square.

The Wildes' house was situated on the north side of the square and this was the oldest and traditionally the most fashionable side. Lady Bracknell would have approved of 1 Merrion Square as an address, given her reservations about the location of Jack Worthing's house on Belgrave Square! When Jack confessed under interrogation by the formidable Lady Bracknell that his address was at No. 149 she replied, 'The unfashionable side. I thought there was something.'[13] William Wilde was a keen book collector and he built up an extensive library containing hundreds of books on a wide range of subjects including poetry, English and continental literature, theatre, classic Greek and Roman authors, Irish history and topography, art and many books on other subjects.

At the heart of fashionable nineteenth-century Dublin, Merrion Square provided the residences of the leading barristers, bankers and doctors of the city as well as members of the aristocracy. The residents entertained on a lavish scale, and William and Jane Wilde were particularly noted for their excellent dinner parties. During the courses, Oscar and his brother were introduced to the distinguished guests and were encouraged to sit quietly and listen to the conversation. In an early interview, Oscar Wilde acknowledged that 'the best of his education in boyhood' was obtained from listening to his father and mother and their remarkable friends: 'Mr Wilde was constantly with his father and mother,' the interviewer reports, 'always among grown up persons, and, at eight years old, had heard every subject discussed and every creed defended and demolished at his father's dinner table, where were to be found not only the brilliant genius of Ireland, but also celebrities of Europe and America that visited Dublin.'[14]

12 Ibid.   13 O. Wilde, *The Importance of Being Earnest* in *Collins Complete Works of Oscar Wilde*, Centenary Edition (Glasgow, 1999), pp 366–419 at p. 369.   14 Anon., 'Oscar Wilde', *The Biograph* 4 (1880), 130–5.

One of the most remarkable families living on Merrion Square was the Stokes family, close neighbours of the Wildes. William Stokes was Regius professor of Medicine at Trinity College and he counted William Wilde among his friends. The Stokes children were encouraged to develop artistic and intellectual interests. Margaret became an artist and an accomplished book illustrator and Whitley became a Celtic scholar and was well known to the Pre-Raphaelites. Matthew Arnold referred to Whitley Stokes in his influential essay 'On the Study of Celtic Literature' as 'one of the very ablest scholars.'[15] Although he was a physician, William Stokes considered it one of his avocations to increase the influence of the arts so that the beautiful could not 'fail to elevate and civilize the human mind'.[16] The family encouraged music, acting and wit. The art historian Anne Crookshank, a descendant of William Stokes, remembers that paradox and wit still formed an integral part of conversation in the Stokes family in her childhood. She recalls an incident when she was a child when she saw her grandmother write two letters and address the envelopes. She then noticed that her grandmother placed one of the letters in the wrong envelope. 'Granny', she said, 'you have just put that letter in the wrong envelope.' 'My dear', replied her grandmother, 'it is the only way of letting people know what you really think of them.'[17] If repartee such as this flourished in Merrion Square, it also seems at home in the world of Oscar Wilde's society plays.

John Pentland Mahaffy, Oscar's tutor at Trinity, was closely connected with the Stokes family through friendship and marriage. Mahaffy greatly admired the conversational skills of William Stokes and he recalled how Stokes delighted in mystifying guests by the use of paradox. Stokes once remarked to the young Mahaffy that an over-insistence on accuracy could spoil good conversation: a precept which Mahaffy later elaborated in his book *The Art of Conversation*, claiming it was even justifiable to tell untruths for the sake of a good story. Oscar went further in his *The Decay of Lying*, which was (in part) a parody of Mahaffy's style, when he declared that 'Lying, the telling of beautiful untrue things, is the proper aim of Art.'[18]

15 M. Arnold, *On the Study of Celtic Literature and on Translating Homer* (London, 1893), p. 63. 16 W. Stokes, 'The Manchester Exhibition of Art Treasures', *Dublin University Magazine* 49 (1857), 608–20. 17 A. Crookshank, Personal Communication (1995). 18 O. Wilde, 'The Decay of Lying' in *Complete Works*, op. cit., pp 1071–92 at pp 1091–2.

Two other leading physicians of the Irish School of Medicine – Robert Graves, and Dominic Corrigan – also lived on Merrion Square. Graves, together with Stokes, championed the development of bedside clinical teaching in the English-speaking world, and their books had considerable influence on the development of medicine in North America. Their names are linked to medical syndromes and are still recalled daily in hospitals throughout the world. They did not confine their interests to medicine. Robert Graves painted with Turner on the Continent, and Sir Dominic Corrigan wrote a book about his travels in Greece.

Every afternoon between two and four o'clock during Oscar Wilde's childhood, carriages would jostle for space outside the houses in Merrion Square, as patients alighted to visit their doctors. Sir Philip Crampton was one of the most distinguished surgeons living on Merrion Square. He was surgeon general to the army in Ireland, consulted at the Meath Hospital and also worked with Wilde in his Eye and Ear Hospital. He lived at 14 Merrion Square and a famous pear tree grew outside the house. He was also a Fellow of the Royal Society and a close friend of the novelist Maria Edgeworth. Sir Walter Scott admired 'the liveliness and range of his talk' when he met Crampton during his tour of Ireland in 1825.[19]

Crampton's love of fine clothes was legendary. A contemporary satirical medical writer referred to Crampton as a dandy in a sketch which was published in *The Lancet* and went on to express amazement that he had recently lectured to his students dressed in a plain suit of black:

> We never, indeed, saw him look better, nor more like one of his own species; for, on other occasions, he seemed to us half bear, half beaver, so completely had the pelts of these animals concealed his human form.[20]

Several of the other leading doctors on Merrion Square were also noted for their elegance. Evory Kennedy was a very distinguished obstetrician and master of the Rotunda Hospital who shared Crampton's enthusiasm for fur. Oscar Wilde would not look out of place in such company.

Speranza decided to hold a weekly salon at her home in Merrion Square. She informed a friend that she and her husband had dined with

19 J.G. Lockhart, *Life of Sir Walter Scott* (Robert Cadell, 1837), p. 57.   20 M. Fallon, *Sketches of Erinensis: Selections of Irish Medical Satire* (London, 1979), p. 65.

four peers within a fortnight, 'all dressed out as fine as peacocks and souls shrivelled as small as sparrows. What miserable twaddle I find myself talking sometimes … I am going to establish weekly conversazione at my own house (if I can) and agglomerate together all the thinking minds of Dublin.'[21] The salon was such a great success that there was often standing room only for the many guests. The Swedish poet and essayist Lotten Von Kraemer recalled a very pleasant evening with the family discussing the legends and history of Sweden. Lotten was very impressed by Speranza and wrote that 'the fire in her gaze betrays the famous poetess whose lofty songs are so beloved in her homeland.'[22]

The Irish playwright Dion Boucicault was another visitor to whom the young Oscar was introduced. Their meeting was to mark the beginning of a friendship which Wilde would later turn to his advantage when setting out on his own literary career. Boucicault was to advise Wilde on the structure of his first play, *Vera*, and, although Wilde eschewed the 'stage Irishness' of his colleague, he was definitely influenced by some of Boucicault's work. For instance Boucicault's play *A Lover by Proxy*, written in 1842, anticipated *The Importance of Being Earnest* (1895) in a number of ways. Harry Lawless and Peter Blushington, two amusing gentlemen of leisure, suggest Jack Worthing and Algernon Moncrieff. There are also similarities between Miss Penelope Prude and Miss Prism and parallels in the garden scenes of both plays.[23]

During the latter half of the nineteenth century, Leinster House on Merrion Square was developed into the cultural nucleus of the city. Leinster House had been acquired by the Royal Dublin Society from the duke of Leinster earlier in the century. In 1853 just two years before the Wildes moved to the square there was a major Industrial Exhibition in the grounds of Leinster House. The temporary building constructed to house the exhibition was known as the Temple of Industry and it covered an area of 6.5 acres. The Great Hall of the exhibition housed a collection of antiquities, contemporary art and a loan exhibition of Old Masters. The success of this exhibition led to the building of the National Gallery in the grounds of Leinster House. The gallery was formally opened by the lord lieutenant, the earl of Carlisle on 30 January 1864, when Oscar was nine

21 J. Wilde Letters, Reading University, No. 22.   22 J. Melville, *Mother of Oscar: Life of Jane Francesca Wilde* (London, 1994), p. 71.   23 D. Krause, *The Profane Book of Irish Comedy* (Ithaca, 1982), p. 186.

years old. A visit to the galleries was an adventure for the young Oscar Wilde. The sculpture gallery was situated in the main hall on the ground floor where casts of Greek and Roman originals were arranged between the Corinthian columns. The collection of the picture gallery, although small at the beginning, included several works by some of the great European masters. Many of the themes were biblical and it is noteworthy in view of Oscar's later interest in Salomé and St John the Baptist that the small collection included no fewer than three paintings of the saint. *The Beheading of John the Baptist* was acquired in 1864 and catalogued as a Caravaggio. However, in 1971 it was identified as the work of the seventeenth-century artist, Mattia Preti.

Wilde's early environment shaped his work in other, unexpected ways. Nineteenth-century travel writers claimed that no city in Europe of proportionate size possessed as many spacious and beautiful squares as Dublin. The Georgian houses of Merrion Square were built around a magnificent garden. Describing the square, a writer of the period observed:

> The interior is enclosed by a lofty iron railing, on a dwarf wall of mountain-granite. Immediately within the railing is a thickly planted and luxuriant shrubbery which gives an air of perfect retirement to the interior walk ... The houses on the north side of the square are some of the best built and most convenient in Dublin: they were built after the design of Mr Ensor; the basement stories of all, on that side, are of mountain-granite and rusticated, and the three upper stories are of brick; the houses on the other sides are entirely of brick. The north side of this square has been a summer promenade for many years.[24]

Today the gardens of Merrion Square are open to the public and there is a playground for children. However, when Oscar was a child these gardens were reserved exclusively for the use of the families living in the square and were entered with a private key. Oscar would have played in these gardens protected, like the happy prince of his fairy tale, from the harsh realities of life outside and in particular from the dreadful slums which were situated directly behind the elegant square.[25]

24 G.N. Wright, *An Historical Guide to Ancient and Modern Dublin* (London, 1821), p. 141.
25 D. Coakley, 'The Neglected Years: Wilde in Dublin' in G. Sandulescu (ed.), *Rediscovering*

In 1864 William Wilde sent his sons Oscar and Willie to Portora Royal School at Enniskillen. Portora enjoyed an excellent reputation and most of the school's pupils were the sons of landed gentry, clergy and professional people. According to the Prize Book of the time Oscar did well at Portora. He came fourth in classics in 1869, obtained third prize for drawing (his brother Willie was second), and he was placed fifth in Holy Scripture. In the following year he won the classical prize, being first in the year, and also won the Carpenter Greek Testament Prize. He was again first in classics in his last year at the school, winning also the assistant master's prize in ancient history and coming second in drawing.[26] He crowned these achievements by being awarded a royal scholarship to study at Trinity College Dublin.

Oscar Wilde found in Trinity an ideal environment for the further development of his talents. The university already had an impressive list of distinguished alumni such as the politicians Edmund Burke and Henry Grattan, the scholars George Berkeley and William Molyneux, and the writers Jonathan Swift and William Congreve. Above all it had produced great talkers and wits, men like Oliver Goldsmith who fascinated London society in the eighteenth century and William Maginn who did the same in the first half of the nineteenth century. Maginn (1793–1842), who was mentioned by Wilde in his essay 'Pen, Pencil and Poison', was in his time one of the dominant talents on the literary landscape of London numbering among his friends figures such as Carlyle and Thackeray. At the pinnacle of his career, William Maginn made a mistake, which Wilde would repeat later in the century, with similar tragic consequences. Maginn took on the might of a leading English aristocratic family, the Berkeleys of Berkeley Castle, when he exposed some of the family's skeletons in an injudicious book review. The result was a duel, followed by a period in a debtors' prison from which he emerged with his spirits completely broken. He died a year after his release in 1843 aged forty-nine.[27]

Why did Trinity produce so many great wits? John Pentland Mahaffy, who was one of the most accomplished talkers of his time, had his own theories:

Oscar Wilde (Gerrards Cross, 1994), pp 52–60.   **26** Merlin Holland, Personal Communication.   **27** M. and D. Coakley, *Wit and Wine* (Dublin, 1985), pp 81–8.

> As Irishmen they are fluent talkers, and as Trinity College men they are independent talkers, free to utter opinions, not guided by precedent, differing readily, even from their teachers. Those Fellows who encourage conversation at their lectures soon make them like the old disputations of the schools ... A man is judged by his conversation, by his ability to take in new ideas.[28]

Although it has been generally accepted that Wilde resided with his parents at 1 Merrion Square during his first year at college, the college register of chambers for the period reveals that Wilde was given rooms in the college in November 1871 and that he continued to occupy these rooms throughout his three years in Trinity.[29] Wilde's rooms were situated in the quadrangle known as Botany Bay, on the first floor of No. 18. Edward Carson, who would confront Wilde at the Old Bailey years later, also entered Trinity in 1871 but did not, like Wilde, take rooms in the college.

Wilde studied under several very able classical scholars and philosophers. These included John Pentland Mahaffy, Thomas Kingsmill Abbot, Robert Yelverton Tyrell, John Kells Ingram and Arthur Palmer. All of these men had reputations which extended far beyond the walls of their own college. Wilde himself acknowledged that both Tyrell and Mahaffy had a major influence on him. Tyrell was a Greek and Latin scholar and he was also admired for his wit. He was the professor of Latin when Wilde joined the university but was later appointed to the chair of Greek. Lord John Ross, who studied classics at Trinity in the 1870s, later wrote that the students looked upon Tyrell 'as an incarnation of an ancient Greek. To read a Sophoclean play with him was a joy past understanding. If ever a man had in him the spirit of Hellas, he had it.' He added that 'Tyrell was a great literary artist and I have never met any person with such genius for the interpretation of Shakespeare.'[30]

John Kells Ingram was professor of Greek when Wilde was at Trinity but it was in the field of political economy that he gained most recognition. He was also a poet and is remembered today as the author of the poem *The Memory of the Dead* ('Who fears to speak of Ninety-Eight')

28 J.P. Mahaffy, 'Life in Trinity College Dublin', *The Dark Blue* 1 (1871), 487–93. 29 Register of Chambers, Library, Trinity College Dublin MUN/V/86/4, pp 207–8. 30 J. Ross, *The Years of My Pilgrimage* (London, 1924), pp 21–2.

which was published in *The Nation* in 1843. He wrote this well known nationalist poem when his sympathies were with the Young Ireland Movement but when Wilde knew him he had withdrawn from political affairs and was concentrating on scholarly pursuits.

An old family friend, John Pentland Mahaffy was professor of Ancient History. Just three years before Wilde arrived in the university, Mahaffy had published his *Twelve Lectures on Primitive Civilisations* and he continued to publish regularly over the following two decades. Mary Colum remembered in her autobiography *Life and the Dream* that 'Mahaffy could talk of Sophocles and Socrates as if he had met them at dinner the night before, where, like Dublin gentlemen, they drank a little too much.'[31] Mahaffy was also an authority on old silver, antique furniture and Georgian architecture. He knew his wines and was an outstanding sportsman. 'Though he could teach history, Greek, German and music at will,' the writer Shane Leslie recalled, 'I knew him best as a snipe-shooter.'[32] Lord John Ross had similar memories of Mahaffy:

> The best known Trinity College man of his time was undoubtedly Dr. Mahaffy, the Professor of Ancient History. He was celebrated as an all-round man. There was nothing he could not do – classics, philosophy, papyrus script reading, architecture, music – while his numerous books on Greek life and thought are in every cultured home. He could play cricket with the best. He was an excellent rifle-shot and, as a game-shot in the covert, or in a snipe bog, few could equal him.[33]

Mahaffy was renowned for his conversational skills and he wrote a book *On the Art of Conversation*. He had several acquaintances amongst the royal and aristocratic families of Europe, and liked to entertain his colleagues in the Common Room at Trinity with anecdotes about these acquaintances. Many of his colleagues believed that these stories were highly embellished. When he recalled that he had been beaten only once as a child and 'that was for telling the truth,' one of them quickly replied, 'It certainly cured you, Mahaffy.'[34] Another of his stories set at a corona-

31 M. Colum, *Life and the Dream* (London, 1947), p. 286.   32 S. Leslie, *The End of a Chapter* (London, 1916), p. 140.   33 J. Ross, *The Years of My Pilgrimage*, op. cit.   34 W.B. Stanford and R.B. McDowell, *Mahaffy* (London, 1971), p. 85.

tion included a paraphrase of Charles V's famous dictum about the languages of Europe. Mahaffy claimed that he was overheard by the Kaiser when chatting to the queen of Spain: 'Madam,' I said, 'Spanish is the language of Kings; French is the language of diplomacy; Italian is the language of love; German I speak to my horse.'[35] Jonathan Swift had used the same Charles V anecdote in *Gulliver's Travels* when describing the language of the highly intelligent horses, the Houynhnms.

Wilde poked fun in a similar way at German in Act II of the *Importance of Being Earnest* when Cecily declares:

> But I don't like German. It isn't at all a becoming language. I know perfectly well that I look quite plain after my German lesson.[36]

Jane Wilde acknowledged that it was Mahaffy who gave the first 'noble impulse to Oscar's intellect.'[37] Mahaffy was well known to the family, a frequent guest at 1 Merrion Square and also Willie Wilde's tutor at Trinity. According to Mahaffy, Oscar was a 'delightful man to talk to on matters of scholarship, his views were always so fresh and unconventional.'[38] Mahaffy, like Wilde in later years, was a great believer in the supernatural and claimed to have seen apparitions on more than one occasion. He enjoyed captivating audiences with ghost stories and relating his own thrilling experiences.[39]

During these undergraduate years at Trinity, Wilde developed his interest in aesthetics and the appreciation of the beautiful. Papers were read on aestheticism at student society meetings. Mahaffy published a book on Kant's philosophy under the title *The Aesthetic and Analytic*. 'Aesthetic' principles had influenced the architecture of one of the most recently erected buildings on the university campus: the Museum Building, completed in 1854 and inspired by the work of John Ruskin. Ruskin would later stimulate Wilde's 'aesthetic' leanings when the latter went to Oxford. It may have been, in part, Oscar's interest in aestheticism which attracted him to Catholicism while at Trinity. He became very friendly with members of the Jesuit order and he attended Mass. Wilde later told his Oxford

35 D.A. Webb (ed.), *Of One Company* (Dublin, 1951), p. 124.   36 O. Wilde, *The Importance of Being Earnest*, in *Complete Works*, op. cit., p. 375.   37 D. Coakley, *Oscar Wilde: The Importance of being Irish*, p. 149.   38 L. Purser, Letter to A.J.A. Symonds, William Andrews Clark Library, University of California (1932).   39 J.G. MacNeill Swift, *What I Have Seen and Heard* (London, 1925), p. 58.

friend, David Hunter Blair, that it was his father's displeasure that kept him from joining the Catholic Church. It has been suggested that it was Oscar's fascination with Catholicism while at Trinity which motivated Sir William Wilde to support his son's transfer to Oxford in 1874.

Oscar had a very good academic record at Trinity. He won a Foundation Scholarship in June 1873 which gave him an annual sum of £20 (a considerable sum in those days) together with several privileges. In 1874 he was awarded the blue ribbon of classical scholarship at Trinity, the Berkeley Gold Medal. In the same year Wilde and another student named H.B. Leech helped Mahaffy with his book *Social Life in Greece*. One of the subjects covered in detail in the book was the fascination which Greek men had for beautiful youths. Mahaffy argued that the driving force behind these relationships was an intellectual one. Wilde would use a similar line of reasoning in his famous reply to the prosecuting counsel at the Old Bailey when asked 'What is the Love that dare not speak its name?'[40]

In 1874 Oscar won a Classical Demyship or scholarship to Magdalen College, Oxford. As a consequence he left Trinity after three years without taking a degree there. During his first year at Oxford he attended Ruskin's lectures on Florentine art in the University Museum building, which like the Museum Building of Trinity had been designed by Benjamin Woodward. Oscar was a mature student at Oxford. From early childhood he would have mixed with highly intellectual and cultured individuals and he was no stranger to aristocratic company. This background made it easy for him to impress his fellow students at Oxford as it would also allow him in later years to move with ease in the highest circles of London society. This has not been understood by many of Wilde's biographers.

Whilst at Oxford, Wilde maintained his links with Ireland by returning during vacation to Merrion Square and by spending several holidays in the West of Ireland at Lough Fee and Lough Corrib where he enjoyed fishing and shooting. He also kept up his friendship with Mahaffy. They toured the north of Italy together in 1875 and a year later Wilde corrected the proofs of Mahaffy's book *Rambles and Studies in Greece* at the professor's country retreat, 'Sealawn',[41] on the Howth Peninsula in north

40 D. Coakley, *Importance of being Irish*, op. cit., p. 156. 41 The house was named Sealawn when Wilde stayed there and not Earlscliff as stated in all Wilde biographies to date. At some time after Mahaffy's occupancy the house was renamed Earlscliff and it is known by

Dublin. During the Easter vacation in 1877 Wilde accompanied Mahaffy on a visit to Greece which extended into term time. 'Now you have been to Greece', Mahaffy advised him after their return, 'go over to London and tell them all about it.'[42]

From their lofty position in Merrion Square society the Wildes affected a disdain for trade. One evening a guest mentioned to Speranza that she would like to bring along a friend on the next occasion, explaining that she was 'respectable.' 'You must never employ that description in this house,' admonished Speranza, 'only trades people are "respectable".'[43] Oscar shared Speranza's opinion on this subject. Edward Saltus, who had known Oscar during his 'aesthetic phase' when he dressed in knee-breeches, wore velvet and had long hair, was surprised when he met him later in London: 'He was married, he was a father, and in his house in Tite Street he seemed a bit bourgeois. Of that he may have been conscious. I remember one of his children running and calling at him: "My good papa!" and I remember Wilde patting the boy and saying: "Don't call me that, it sounds so respectable".'[44]

Yet is it possible that the Wildes had something to conceal in their family background and that there could have been some 'respectable' skeletons hidden in the cupboards of Merrion Square. William Wilde's father Thomas Wilde was a general practitioner in Castlerea in the west of Ireland and his father, Ralph Wilde, was a landowner and also agent for the local landlord Lord Mount Sandford. Ralph's origins however have remained obscure; some biographers claim that he was descended from a Colonel De Wilde, who is said to have been a Dutch army officer who served in the army of William of Orange during his campaigns in Ireland and was supposed to have been granted land in Connacht as a reward for his services. Other biographers claim that Ralph Wilde was descended from builders who came from Wolsingham, a town in Durham, in the middle of the eighteenth century.

By far the most scholarly study of Wilde's ancestry to date was carried out by Brian de Breffny in 1972.[45] His findings indicated that Ralph was

this name today.   **42** O. Gogarty, *As I Was going down Sackville Street: A Phantasy in Fact* (London, 1937), p. 238.   **43** H. Wyndham, *Speranza: A Biography of Lady Wilde* (London, 1951), p. 70.   **44** E. Saltus, *Oscar Wilde. An Idler's Impressions* (Chicago, 1917), p. 15. **45** B. de Breffny, 'The Paternal Ancestry of Oscar Wilde', *Irish Ancestor* 4.2 (1972), 96–9.

most probably a son of a Dublin merchant named John Wilde who belonged to a family of merchants, ironmongers and property developers. So it would appear that the Wildes of Merrion Square were descended from people with a background in trade. Further support for this belief comes from an article about William Wilde which was published in *Duffy's Hibernian Magazine* in 1864 when the surgeon was awarded his knighthood. It is clear that whoever wrote the anonymous article in the magazine knew the Wilde family very well. The article was written from a nationalist perspective and in stressing William Wilde's Irish credentials the author mentioned a member of the Wilde family, Richard Wilde, who was a United Irishman and who had emigrated to America in 1796. 'Another of the family, a man of high commercial standing in Dublin, became a United Irishman, and fled to America in '98, where, however, his son became Chief Justice, and well known in literature by his graceful "Life of Tasso" and many other works.'[46]

Richard Wilde was an Ironmonger and hardware merchant, originally at 12 High Street and later at 73 Thomas Street. Richard's son, Richard Henry Wilde, was a poet, writer, lawyer and politician.[47] He represented the state of Georgia in the United States congress. One of his poems, 'My life is like the Summer rose' can be found in most anthologies of nineteenth-century American verse. In 1835 he travelled to Florence where he researched and wrote a book on Tasso which was published in 1842.[48] In the course of his research in the archives of the grand duke of Tuscany he came upon a reference to a lost portrait of Dante in the Bargello which had been attributed to Giotto.[49] Wilde's enthusiasm played a key role in initiating a search in the Bargello where the painting was found under a whitewashed wall.[50] The painting can still be seen today and is thought to be the work of the school of Giotto rather than Giotto himself. This has proven to be the earliest portrait of Dante on which all subsequent portraits have been based. Richard Henry Wilde's part in this discovery made

46 Anon., 'Sir William Wilde', *Duffy's Hibernian Sixpenny Magazine* 5, pp 201–3.   47 E.L. Tucker, *Richard Henry Wilde: His Life and Selected Poems* (Athens, 1966).   48 R.H. Wilde, *Conjectures and Researches concerning the Love, Madness and Imprisonment of Torquato Tasso* (New York, 1842).   49 T.W. Koch, *Dante in America* (Boston, 1896), pp 23–36.   50 R.T. Holbrook, *Portraits of Dante, from Giotto to Raphael* (New York, 1911), pp 73–150; P. Barocchi, G.G. Bertelá, *Dal Ritratto di Dante alla Mostra del Medio Evo* 2 (Firenze, 1840–65), p. 4; B. Tomasello, *Il Museo del Bargello* (Firenze, 1998), p. 58.

him a celebrity in the United States. He once prophetically remarked that the name Wilde was an unusual one and that he had a premonition that one day it would 'make a noise in the world.'[51] The fact that the Wildes of Merrion Square claimed Richard Henry Wilde as kin is further evidence of the family connection with the eighteenth-century Dublin merchants.

It is ironical that Oscar Wilde, who is often described as not being really Irish, has after all a better right to be proclaimed as a genuine Dubliner than many other writers portrayed as such. At least, we can now be confident that we know a secret about the Wildes of Merrion Square which they guarded carefully during their lifetimes – that there was after all a connection with trade, or as Lady Bracknell would say 'with the purple of commerce.'

---

51 E.L. Tucker, *Richard Henry Wilde*, op. cit., p.1.

Sir William Wilde, 1815–1876: demographer and Irish medical historian

PETER FROGGATT

I

Oscar's parents were significant figures in their own right. The *Dictionary of National Biography* of 1900 gives them two columns. Neither had by then attracted a biographer and they were soon eclipsed by Oscar's fame and notoriety. Sir William in fact became little more than a footnote in Wildean studies, a shadowy figure from the medical *haut monde* of Victorian Dublin, dimly remembered, if at all, for licentiousness rather than anything edifying. His rehabilitation started in 1942 with T.G. Wilson's biography[1] and is now complete. This is no more than justice because even by the larger-than-life Victorian standards Wilde was a remarkable polymath worthily credited with no less than ten avocations which are listed on the memorial plaque on his house at No. 1 Merrion Square; I will be dealing with just two of the ten, his work as a demographer and as a medical historian.

On 28th January 1864 the Most Illustrious Order of St Patrick held a chapter meeting in the great public rooms at Dublin Castle. The lord lieutenant, the earl of Carlisle, who was grand master of the Order, invested the up-and-coming Lord Dufferin as the newest of the Order's twenty-two knight companions. He then dissolved the meeting and from the throne called forward the forty-eight-year-old William Wilde. Carlisle:

> conferred the honour of knighthood on Mr W.R. Wilde and addressing him observed "I do so, not so much in honour of your

---

[1] Unless otherwise noted, facts may be found in the following standard texts: T.G. Wilson, *Victorian Doctor; being the Life of Sir William Wilde* (London, 1942); T. de Vere White, *The Parents of Oscar Wilde: Sir William and Lady Wilde* (London, 1967); R. Ellmann, *Oscar Wilde* (London, 1987); and D. Coakley, *Oscar Wilde: The Importance of being Irish* (Dublin, 1994).

high professional reputation, but to mark my appreciation of your services to statistical science, and especially in connexion with the Irish census".[2]

This was the pinnacle of Wilde's career. His census work, that monumental labour of love, was at long last officially and explicitly recognized. But even as he knelt before the throne, clouds of imputation and scandal were gathering which together with the deaths of his three daughters – Isola in 1867 aged nine, and his natural daughters Mary and Emily in 1871 aged respectively twenty-two and twenty-four – were to darken his closing years.

Uncertainty surrounds the Wilde family's provenance. We know, however, that William's grandfather, Ralph, settled in Castlerea in Co. Roscommon in the 1750s where he is variously described over the next twenty years as 'dealer', then 'farmer', and finally 'gentleman' – an impeccable progression: in reality he was Lord Mount Sandford's local agent. His eldest son, also Ralph, won the Berkeley Gold Medal in Greek at Trinity College Dublin as his grandnephew Oscar was to do nearly a century later. Ralph senior's second son, Thomas, married in 1796 Emily (or Amelia) Fynne of a Mayo family then living in Dublin, and they had two daughters and three sons, William, my subject, born in the townland of Kilkeevin, Castlerea, in March 1815 being the youngest.[3] Both of William's brothers, John and yet another Ralph, entered Holy Orders and appear later in William's life: John (then incumbent of Trinity Church, Norwich) officiated at William's wed-

---

2 *Dublin Journal of Medical Science* 37.74 (1864), 379.   3 Thomas received the Doctor of Medicine (MD) degree of the University of St Andrews on 27 January 1809 by the then usual method of a recommendation from two other MDs (of any university) and the payment of a fee commonly of some £25. Thomas' two sponsors were James Cleghorn MD, sometime president of the King's and Queen's College of Physicians of Ireland, and John Pentland MD, of Dublin, who attested that he had 'attended and completed a course of Lectures on the General Branches of Medicine in Trinity College Dublin, has received a Liberal Education, is a Respectable Character, and from personal knowledge we judge him worthy of the honour of a degree in Medicine.' He had no other qualifications. He died on 1 January 1838 aged 78 and is buried in Holy Trinity Church of Ireland graveyard, Castlerea, his tombstone stating that 'he practised as a Physician in this town for upwards of 30 years' (i.e. from the time of the award of his MD). What he did and where he did it before 1809 is unknown. I am indebted to Mr Fergus O'Connor FRCS, ophthalmic surgeon, Bury, and Dr Norman Reid, Keeper of Manuscripts and Monuments, University of St Andrews, for unpublished facts about Sir William's father's medical qualifications.

ding on 12 November 1851 at St Peter's, Dublin; and Ralph (then rector of Kilsallaghan) christened Oscar at St Mark's, Dublin on 26 April 1855, and also was to adopt William's two natural daughters.

William attended the Royal School, Banagher, and the Diocesan School at Elphin. He came to Dublin in 1832 aged seventeen and studied at Park Street Medical School (in what is now Lincoln Place); later it became the final site of his own St Mark's Ophthalmic Hospital, and later still the department of genetics at Trinity until its recent demolition. He was apprenticed to Abraham Colles at Dr Steevens' Hospital, then interned briefly at the Rotunda Lying-in Hospital, and finally received his letters testimonial – that is his 'licence' – from the Royal College of Surgeons in Ireland on 13 March 1837. But he was unwell – he had nearly died of typhus – and for convalescence, and probably also to keep him from entering the obscurity of country practice, his seniors appointed him curator of the hospital's museum and after that arranged for him to accompany a wealthy tubercular Glaswegian (Robert Meiklam) and his wife on a cruise to Madeira, the Canaries and the Mediterranean. They sailed from the Isle of Wight on 24 September 1837 on Meiklam's 130-ton steam yacht the RYS *Crusader*. Wilde was then twenty-two. T.G. Wilson describes him:

> Short … and slender with a pale, oval face framed in black hair worn long … His forehead was lofty, but narrow, his pale eyes were somewhat prominent … The nose was long, straight and well-shaped … The mouth was wide with sensuous lips … the chin was long and receding … A face which reflected the more voluptuous side of its owner's nature but gave little indication of his brilliant intellect and still less of his determination of character.[4]

He had boundless energy, a sharp eye, and an impressive intellect, an enquiring mind, and revelled in the cruise – clambering over Madeira and Tenerife, scampering up the pyramids, visiting Egyptian medical schools and hospitals, and trudging the Holy Land; and missing absolutely nothing. And forever writing his diary and ream after ream of notes.

He returned to Dublin in June 1838 after nine months and took rooms at 199 Great Brunswick Street (now Pearse Street). While waiting for

4 T.G. Wilson, *Victorian Doctor*, op. cit., p. 15.

patients he did what Drs Arthur Conan Doyle and A. J. Cronin were later to do – he wrote. Mainly it was the two-volume science-travel best-seller of the cruise[5] for a very welcome author's fee of £250, but he also wrote articles, talks and lectures which earned him precocious membership of the Royal Irish Academy in June 1839 aged only twenty-four. His writing also won him an impressive public, including the talented coterie at the *Dublin University Magazine*, and the power-brokers at the Castle and at the Ordnance Survey who would soon put his talents to good use.

Though other callings beckoned, Wilde was decided on a career as an eye and ear surgeon and in July 1839 he left to study at the customary centres – Moorfields Hospital in London, then the Allgemeines Krankenhaus in Vienna where he collected material for another successful book,[6] then to Munich, Prague, Dresden, Heidelberg and Berlin, and finally back to Dublin in the spring of 1841, some twenty months later. While in London he wrote the first of his biographical 'Memoirs' which were to be a significant feature of his historical output: it was of Sir Thomas Molyneux, the first Irish medical baronet. Wilde saw something of himself in Molyneux, observing that

> [Molyneux] was [a man] who to the highest professional attainments and the most extensive practice in his calling added a well-deserved reputation in general literature, natural history, and antiquities.[7]

At that time Wilde would have asked for no more fitting an epitaph for himself.

II

The Census Commissioners, led by Thomas Larcom, now sought Wilde's services. The recently instituted (1839) Registrar-General's Reports in

5 W.R. Wilde, *Narrative of a Voyage to Madeira, Teneriffe, and along the Shores of the Mediterranean* (Dublin, 1839). 6 W.R. Wilde, *Austria: Its Literary, Scientific, and Medical Institutions, with Notes upon the Present State of Science, and a Guide to the Hospitals and Sanitary Institutions of Vienna* (Dublin, 1843). 7 W.R. Wilde, 'Gallery of Illustrious Irishmen – No. XIII: Sir Thomas Molyneux, Bart., MD, FRS', *Dublin University Magazine* 18 (Sept. 1841), 305–27, at p. 305.

England and Wales, which had no parallel in Ireland, placed a political imperative on the Commissioners to analyse the causes of deaths ascertained at the census. They offered the job and £315 to Wilde, who leapt at the offer despite his professional commitments; and his landmark *Report upon the Causes of Death* was published two years later to wide acclaim,[8] as the *Dublin Journal of Medical Science* said, 'doing him infinite merit both as to the mode adopted for obtaining accurate results, and the labour and extreme care bestowed.'[9] It ran to 205 pages of tables and seventy-eight foolscap pages of commentary and competed for Wilde's time with his burgeoning professional practice, his heavy lecture load, his hospital and dispensary duties, his archaeological and antiquarian work through the Royal Irish Academy, the publication of his book on Austria, and other writings, and an energetic social life. Does his *Report* then deserve its plaudits, and if so why?

Wilde started by preparing a 94–item classification of fatal diseases. It was modelled on that created in England by William Farr (Compiler of Abstracts at the General Register Office, actually the *de facto* Registrar-General), but included Irish terminology based on deep research on sources including old unpublished MSS. Wilde then examined the 1,187,374 deaths enumerated as having occurred in Ireland since the last census (of 1831) ten years before to see if there were associations with the usual suspects – age, sex, domicile, occupation, poverty and so on. For this he used some ingenious methodology and his lengthy commentary showed that he understood the basis of statistical principles.

Is Wilde's work flawless? Strictly speaking, not quite. By this time Friendly Society and Life Assurance actuaries were revolutionizing mortality and morbidity analysis and the Irish Tontine had been a familiar drawing-room topic for a century. Wilde seems unconcerned (or possibly unfamiliar) with these developments. He quotes those seminal pioneers, Captain John Graunt and Sir William Petty from the seventeenth century, and Thomas Short and the Irishman, John Rutty, from the eighteenth; but little from later than 1770.

8 W.R. Wilde, *Report of Commissioners (Ireland)*, H.C. 1843 [504] XXIV, pp 1 *et seq.* 9 Editor, *Dublin Journal of Medical Science* 25 (1844) quoted in P. Froggatt, 'Sir William Wilde, 1815–1876. A Centenary Appreciation: Wilde's Place in Medicine', *Proceedings of the Royal Irish Academy* 77c.10 (Sept. 1977), 261–78 at p. 265.

If this is a flaw it is only so to the pedantic scholar. A young surgeon no matter how broad his interests could not reasonably be *au fait* with the latest work of actuary and mathematician, and the Irish tontine had vanished before Wilde was born. Wilde was (perhaps fortunately) not a free-wheeling Sir William Petty who generalized his medical statistical findings into other fields especially those conducive to his own personal advantage and enrichment, incidentally making his fortune and allowing him to found the great Lansdowne dynasty. However, the lack of interest in these aspects of statistics hints at a potential weakness in Wilde's scholarship – an eclecticism dictated by his exuberant enthusiasms rather than by dispassionate objectivity, and only his genius and instinctive flair often saved him from his critics. And how exciting he makes it all sound. Listen to this as an example of his eloquent, rhythmic and rhapsodical style. It refers to the Famine:

> The great convulsion which society of all grades here has lately experienced, the failure of the potato crop, pestilence, famine, and a most unparalleled extent of emigration, together with bankrupt landlords, pauperising poor-laws, grinding officials, and decimating workhouses, have broken up the very foundations of social intercourse, have swept away the established theories of political economists, and uprooted many of our long-cherished opinions … All the domestic usages of life have been outraged; the tenderest bonds of kindred have been severed, some of the noblest and holiest feelings of human nature have been blotted from the heart, and many of the finest yet firmest links which united the various classes in the community have been rudely burst asunder. Even the ceremonial of religion has been neglected, and the very rites of sepulture, the most sacred and enduring of all the tributes of affection or respect, have been neglected or forgotten; the dead body has rotted where it fell, or formed a scanty meal for the famished dogs of the vicinity, or has been thrown, without prayer or mourning, into the adjoining ditch.

And now the romantic dimension:

> The hum of the spinning-wheel has long ceased to form an accompaniment to the colleen's song; and that song itself, so sweet and

fresh in cabin, field or byre, has scarcely left an echo in our Glens or among the hamlets of our land.[10]

Be that as it may, his work on the censuses (of 1841, 1851, 1861 and 1871) moved the thrust of their central enquiry away from the channel of *Staatenkunde* (that is, statistics as part of the general description of a country) into the channel of disease causation and 'political arithmetic' (that is the art of reasoning by figures upon things relating to the responsibilities of government) which increasingly included life and death. His book on Austria is stuffed with statistics including such nuggets as the information that, in the Allgemeines Krankenhaus, some 6,250 articles were washed daily and an extension opened in 1834 cost exactly £49,183 17s. 5d.! These were not mere numerical arcana to Wilde but meaningful proxies for more comprehensive descriptions. He had a rare instinct for quantitative methods but was no slave to them. He used statistics; statistics didn't use him.

On 9 October 1850, Wilde was appointed Assistant Commissioner for the 1851 census, 'because', said Lord Clarendon, the lord lieutenant, 'I am aware that you are the person best qualified for it in the country.'[11] But it was a very different Wilde to the 1841 model. He was now, at thirty-five, close to the height of his powers and at the centre of the remarkable Dublin milieu of gifted medical men who were not exclusively medical. Many of them lived in the environs of Merrion Square, highly convenient for Wilde who had just moved from No. 15 Westland Row to the larger No. 21 after his mother's death; it was only a few minutes walk to St Mark's Hospital, the Royal Irish Academy, and most of his other haunts. His hospital was renowned; his reputation was international. He was involved in the administrative offshoots of government through the census and ordnance survey offices and his friendship with Sir Thomas Larcom who was prominent in both. He was active in the statistical and public health movements and was a founder member of the Dublin Statistical Society in 1847.[12] He had now become one of the coterie around the *Dublin University Magazine* and other literary outlets. He had piloted the *Dublin Quarterly Journal of*

10 W.R. Wilde, *Irish Popular Superstitions* (Dublin, 1852), pp 9–10.   11 For facts on Wilde's work on the censuses see P. Froggatt, 'The Demographic Work of Sir William Wilde', *Irish Journal of Medical Science* 6 series VI (May 1965), 213–30; and 'Sir William Wilde and the 1851 Census of Ireland', *Medical History* 9 (Oct. 1965), 302–27.   12 R.D.C. Black, *The Statistical and Social Inquiry Society of Ireland. Centenary Volume, 1847–1947* (Dublin, 1947),

Medical Science (DJMS) into international seas through his editorial fore-sight, energy, skill and his numerous personal contributions. He was one of a group of significant antiquarians and naturalists at the Royal Irish Academy. Within the year he was married and with Speranza would preside over one of the most celebrated *salons* in Dublin.

Wilde had been much moved by the catastrophe of the Famine, as the extract quoted earlier shows, and in 1849 had organized a nation-wide sur-vey and published the results in the *DJMS* in four instalments covering 280 pages.[13] He was a champion of the medical profession – which in 1847 alone lost nearly 200 members, at least 130 from 'fever' contracted while doing their duty[14] – and he supported his colleagues in many ways. He resolved to make the post-Famine 1851 census even more comprehensive than that of 1841, and had ready allies at the Castle. He also wanted to fur-ther his ambitious idea – a national survey of the sick and the handicapped.

The census itself was a Herculean effort with Wilde as the driving force. The results were published in ten foolscap volumes totalling 4,533 pages. The text of three of these volumes was written solely by Wilde, and he had a large hand in a fourth.[15] Two of these volumes, entitled *The Tables of Death*, contained the mortality results as in 1841 but much expanded, while in over 300 pages, he recorded the history of natural catastrophes in Ireland from earliest times.[16] I will return to this remarkable catalogue later. The third volume which he wrote himself was called *The Status of Disease*, and contains the handicap and sickness statistics. Of the handicaps, deaf-dumb-ness was of course (given his medical speciality) his main interest; but he did not just count cases; he wanted to elucidate causes. This led him to a fam-ily study in depth, and this needed a second, or supplementary, census. The method was simple. The main census schedule asked every house-holder to

p. 2; J. McGeachie, '"Normal" Development in an "Abnormal" Place: Sir William Wilde and the Irish School of Medicine' in Greta Jones and Elizabeth Malcolm (eds), *Medicine, Disease and the State in Ireland, 1650–1940* (Cork, 1999), pp 85–101, at pp 86–7. **13** W.R. Wilde, 'Report upon the recent Epidemic Fever in Ireland', *Dublin Journal of Medical Science* 7.13 (Feb. 1849), 64–126; 7.14 (May 1849), 340–404; 8.15 (Aug. 1849), 1–86; 8.16 (Nov. 1849), 270–339. **14** P. Froggatt, 'The Response of the Medical Profession to the Great Famine' in E. M. Crawford (ed.), *Famine: The Irish Experience, 900–1900: Subsistence Crises and Famines in Ireland* (Edinburgh, 1989), pp 134–56, at pp 148–9. **15** See note 11. **16** Census of Ireland 1851, Part V (vols. I and II); Tables of Deaths, *Accounts and Papers (Ireland)*, H.C. 1856 [2087–I], XXIX, pp 261 *et seq.*; 1856 [2087–II], XXX, pp 1 *et seq.*

enter anyone in the house on census night – 30 March 1851 – who was thought to be deaf-and-dumb, and the same information was requested from heads of resident institutions. This yielded 5,680 suspected deaf-and-dumb. Each of these families was now visited and a special nine-question form completed. This pioneer methodology has come to be called 'the double trawl' – the main, then a supplementary census, common now but unusual then and unique in its ambitious scale.

The supplementary nine-question form is remarkably modern; nearly every question would be on a present-day study. Here is none of Wilde's rhapsodical flights into lyrical prose but hard-nosed research using a design ahead of its time. Wilde performed many corroborating medical examinations himself and asked local practitioners to do others, and they rarely refused although it was done *gratis*.

Some of the data are of course suspect since they depend on the knowledge, memory, and veracity of often illiterate householders frequently hostile after their calamities in the greatest disaster in modern Irish history. Wilde personally scrutinised the returns and corrected obvious errors – as when an enumerator entered as deaf-and-dumb every infant under one year of age because they couldn't speak! Errors remain – but this does not detract from Wilde's methodology of the 'double trawl.' He was justly proud of his work 'which has been pronounced by the Press and by the best authorities to be in many respects unsurpassed in Europe.'[17] It was not the first European census of the deaf-and-dumb – Wilde himself referred to the 'magnificent work of Sauveur' in the 1835 Belgian census and nearly forty years ago I was personally able to tabulate twenty-seven such censuses in Europe before Wilde, but most were small, local, involved parts of the many German states and were simply 'counting' exercises often undertaken through Church authorities. Wilde's was by far the biggest and best.[18]

Were Wilde's interpretations rigorous, or did they lean to romanticism? It was of course well known that certain characteristics could 'run in families!' But the family pattern of most cases of congenital deafness is irregular, even quixotic. We now know that this is to be expected with some

17 Letter from Wilde to chief secretary, 12 Nov. 1856, *State Paper Office, C.S.O. Reg. Papers* (1882), No. 43571.   **18** See note 11.

types of so-called Mendelian inheritance. But Mendel was far in the future. Wilde focused on the family patterns, and also whether there was consanguinity (marriage of blood relatives) among the parents of the deaf persons. On both of these he was unequivocal: he wrote, 'an hereditary taint or family peculiarity is manifest in the Irish returns',[19] and of the blood inter-marriage he wrote, 'among the predisposing causes of mu-teism, the too close consanguinity of parents may be looked upon as para-mount.'[20] On each of these he was shown later to be correct.

Finally, did Wilde have any insight into the mechanisms of inheritance of congenital deafness? This is an intriguing question. With Wilde it is tan-talisingly difficult to know which facts he gathered for their innate rele-vance, and which were the result of mere fact collecting for its own sake – which was his greatest obsession. Copious material often from ancient Irish sources is packed into generous footnotes in all his writings, yet in his long dissertation in this great deafness census he quotes *very few relevant contem-porary sources*. Only two years later the great German authority, Meissner, was able to compile no less than fifty-three pages of references in his mon-umental *Taubstummheit und Taubstummenbildung*, and many of them would have been pertinent to Wilde's study![21] At times Wilde seems to anti-cipate the importance of sibship analysis – which had its heyday fifty years later; at other times he flirts with the possible biological significance of deaf-ness occurring in similar twins. In the end, he merely says: 'The trans-mission of disease by hereditary taint or family peculiarity ... is very man-ifest among the deaf and dumb; but like most of the circumstances attend-ing the peculiarities of that class, it is obscure and difficult to be accounted for.'[22] This is admirable if unusual circumspection and his measured con-clusion would probably have been the same if he had read *all* of Meissner's fifty-three pages of references. His intuitive genius was triumphant once again. Today the 1851 census ranks as one of the great national socio-med-ical enquiries of the nineteenth century; and much of it is due to Wilde.

A final comment on Wilde's methodology. I don't think it altogether fanciful to cast him as a quasi-Benthamite; after all, his procedure of, first,

19 W.R. Wilde, *Report on the Status of Disease from the 1851 Census of Ireland*, H.C. 1854 [1765] LVIII, p. 18 and Table IX. **20** W.R. Wilde, *Practical Observations on Aural Surgery and the Nature and Treatment of Diseases of the Ear* (London, 1853), p. 470. **21** F.L. Meissner, *Taubstummheit und Taubstummenbildung* (Leipzig and Heidelberg, 1856). **22** W.R. Wilde, *Practical Observations*, op. cit., p. 472.

systemisation, then fact-gathering, ordering, analysis and deduction, and finally pointers to executive action, is Jeremy Bentham's approved sequencing. And a form of proto-Benthamism *is* evident in Irish administrative practice from the turn of the century – at least in the opinion of the historian Oliver MacDonagh.[23] Or perhaps Wilde was just an unusually rigorous statist? He could have been either, neither or both! Here is a delicious, intellectual problem which I am happy to leave to others.

III

I now turn more briefly to Wilde's credentials as an *Irish* medical historian – I stress *Irish* because he has no wider claim. 'Historian' can be a Humpty-Dumpty word. Applied to a Gibbon or a Runciman it denotes one who describes and dissects the fortunes of great civilizations – as they did. This was not Wilde's scene. To Macauley, a 'historian' composes felicitous narratives and adroitly fashions and disseminates political points of view – as he did. This was not Wilde's scene either. To others, a 'historian' basically describes what happened: the French 'histoire' and the German 'Geschichte' after all mean both 'history' and a 'story.' This was closer, but not quite Wilde either. All agree, however, that so-called 'amateur' historians are best employed in collecting facts which can allow them to tell a story – a biographical memoir perhaps, or the story of an institution – or to provide a reservoir from which professionals can draw in furthering their higher aims of analysis, interpretation and revision. This is far closer to Wilde, but is too narrow a description for his historian's talents. He certainly collected facts, amassed them with a passion bordering on mania; but he used them with great skill in his fluent prose on a wide range of topics. He moved from antiquarian Ireland with its ancient tribes and forgotten battles, its primitive medicines and miraculous cures, its social *mores* and superstitions, and its tangible relics, to more recent events and to histories of Irish medical men and institutions and such arcana as oxen in Ireland[24] and the origins of bog butter.[25] It was narrative history,

23 O. MacDonagh, *The Inspector General: Sir Jeremiah Fitzpatrick and Social Reform, 1783–1802* (London, 1981), chap. 13.   24 W.R. Wilde, 'On the Ancient and Modern Races of Oxen in Ireland', *Proceedings of the Royal Irish Academy* 7 (14 June 1858), 64–75.   25 W.R. Wilde, 'Introduction and the Time of the General Use of the Potato in Ireland and its var-

and it was patriotic in the sense of being founded on love of country and its people. And it was *always* Ireland; in 1846 he expressed his conviction well in a revealing passage:

> The abstract philosopher, or the mere observer and arranger of practical facts, may ask what benefit I confer by the revival and transmission of matters such as I have done. For such [people] I have not written this piece … [however] to those … who sympathise and feel an interest in every department of our country's history, I would say, that, to merit their approbation, I have collected the facts put forward in the previous pages … I would say that no matter how the early political history of our native land may be darkened; of her literacy and scientific history, her monuments, and her antiquities, we have all, as Irishmen, a just right to glow with honest pride![26]

There was therefore method in his mania for collecting facts, a purpose in his pursuit of them. He was not 'the mere observer and arranger of practical facts', though he was certainly all that; not simply a story-teller peddling nostalgia; but he can fairly be said to indulge in loftier historical pursuits and straddle the gulf between 'amateur' and 'professional', a claim enhanced by his talent for lucid description and word-picturing. Here is one picture of which Dickens would have been proud – the Irish barony constables. Wilde writes:

> [they were] generally superannuated pensioners from the yeomanry or militia: always Protestants and most of them foresters, *cleevins*, old servants, or hangers-on of the magistrate – who dressed in long blue surtout coats, with scarlet collars, buckskin breeches, and rusty top-boots. Each of these old men was mounted, and carried a heavy cavalry sword, his only weapon, for he was seldom fit to be entrusted with any other. Two or three of these *fogies* might be seen

ious Failures since that Period, with some Notice of the Substance called Bog Butter', *Proceedings of the Royal Irish Academy* 6 (26 May 1856), 356–72. **26** W.R. Wilde, 'The Editor's Preface: The History of Periodic Medical Literature in Ireland, including Notices of the Medical and Philosophical Societies of Dublin', *Dublin Journal of Medical Science* New Series 1 (Feb. 1846), i-xlix.

at fairs, patterns and markets, riding up and down to keep the peace which, as soon as the superintending magistrate had gone to dinner, they then generally broke by getting gloriously drunk.[27]

Wilde had two major techniques for promulgating the history of Irish medicine: the biographical memoir, and the block-buster catalogue of events. He had a third one, namely, his chronicling of Irish superstitions and antiquities, but these really fall into folklore and antiquarianism. His first biographical memoir was written when he was at Moorfields Hospital in 1839–40. It was of Sir Thomas Molyneux MD – mentioned earlier – it ran to seventy-seven pages, and was published in episodes like the early work of Dickens.[28] Others followed – Sylvester O'Halloran, Sir Patrick Dun, Bartholomew Mosse, John Rutty, Charles Willoughby, David Mac-Bride, John Oliver Curran, Sir Henry Marsh, Sir Robert Kane, William Stokes, Robert Graves, among others[29] – all significant figures in Irish medicine and all, like Wilde himself, with multiple interests and achievements. There were non-medicals as well, such as Dean Swift and Gabriel Beranger, and the colourful rake George Robert Fitzgerald, dubbed 'the fighting Fitzgerald' for his alleged twenty-six duels, who finished on the scaffold.[30] But in truth Wilde was not a particularly good biographer: he was discursive and unfocused and his subject was often submerged under a torrent of loosely deployed facts. We must look in preference to his block-buster compilations.

The best example of these, and the only one I have time to describe is the one I have mentioned – the 300 plus page catalogue of 'pestilences, cosmical phenomena, epizootics and famines' in Ireland from pre-history with summaries of events and sources. This dominated Volume I of Part V of the 1851 census and to complete it, as Wilde wrote, 'I gave up all society and recreation for eighteen months [November 1854 to May 1856, which included the move from Westland Row to Merrion Square] and more than once impaired my health by the incessant daily and nightly labour devoted to this voluminous work.'[31]

27 W.R. Wilde, *Irish Popular Superstitions*, op. cit., p. 83. 28 W.R. Wilde, 'Gallery of Illustrious Irishmen', op. cit. 29 J.B. Lyons, 'Sir William Wilde, 1815–1876', *Journal of the Irish Colleges of Physicians and Surgeons* 5.4 (April 1976), 147–52. 30 W.R. Wilde, *The Life and Times of George Robert Fitzgerald ('Fighting Fitzgerald')* (Dublin, 1851). 31 See note 17.

Wilde decided on a tabular format with dates, phenomena, reported outcomes, associated events, and provenance and authority. The work is the product of prodigious industry, impressive scholarship, and unremitting focus. Clerks and amanuenses – and perhaps even what we would now call research assistants – helped (and we know that some of the census clerks worked in Wilde's house and were paid directly by Wilde) but much of the work and all the responsibility was Wilde's alone. It is not without flaws. All sources, some dubious, are given equal authority. The references are frequently imprecise. The whole presentation is awash with facts undiscerningly presented. But there is an exuberant enthusiasm throughout, and the whole in concept represents a boundless sweep though the Irish experience. It is now a useful source, and to some something indeed of a *curio*, rather than possessing the deeper value which the author intended. Fundamentally, it epitomizes Wilde.

IV

On 12 December 1864, ten months after being knighted, and while completing his work on the 1861 census, Wilde found himself in court in a civil case which 'shook Dublin like a thunderclap' – or more precisely it was Speranza who was in court on a summons that a letter she had written to Dr Robert Travers, Assistant Librarian at Marsh's Library and sometime lecturer in forensic medicine at Trinity, was a libel on the chastity of Travers' semi-estranged daughter, Mary Josephine. The letter complained of Mary Josephine's 'disreputable conduct … in consorting with all the low newspaper boys in Bray',[32] and much else besides; but it fell into Mary Josephine's hands and she at once started proceedings. Wilde himself did not appear in court though joined with his wife in the suit since a husband was then assumed responsible for his wife's torts – an assumption which allowed Mr Bumble in *Oliver Twist* to memorably call the law 'a ass' and 'a idiot' – but all Dublin knew that William Wilde was the real defendant. Mary Josephine had become a patient of Wilde's ten years before and an intimate relationship followed, which endured. When the friendship finally cooled Wilde decided to get rid of her. He tried to buy

32 *Dublin Evening Mail*, 12 Dec. 1864.

1 Philip Crampton

2 Evory Kennedy

3 William Wilde and
William Stokes

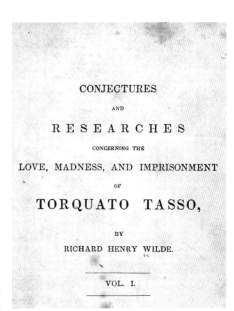

CONJECTURES

AND

RESEARCHES

CONCERNING THE

LOVE, MADNESS, AND IMPRISONMENT

OF

TORQUATO TASSO,

BY

RICHARD HENRY WILDE.

VOL. I.

4 Title page from
R.H. Wilde's book on Tasso

5 Richard Henry Wilde

6 William Wilde

7 Sir William Wilde in later life

8 'Speranza', Lady Wilde

IRELAND'S EYE

A WILDE (K) NIGHT IN IRELAND'S EYE.

9 Cartoon drawing of
Provost John Pentland Mahaffy

10 Cartoon drawing of Sir
William Wilde

11 Plaque to Sir William Wilde at No. 1, Merrion Square, Dublin

12 Oscar Wilde in 1881

her off with presents which she accepted, but they made no difference to her behaviour. He then advised her for her health to join her brothers in Australia and bought her a ticket – a one-way ticket. She accepted the ticket, enjoyed the trip to Liverpool, and enjoyed even more the return to Dublin the next day. Wilde then allegedly offered to escort her to Liverpool and see her off on the Australia boat. She rejected the offer of escort, again took the passage money, went to Liverpool, saw the boat off herself, and returned again to Dublin. Wilde finally discarded her and she started to attack him in scurrilous doggerel in the press and offensive pamphlets publicly distributed. These eventually exhausted Speranza's patience and prompted the letter to Dr Travers. The details which the plaintiff alleged in court cast Wilde as a promiscuous voluptuary who took advantage of his professional position to satisfy his lusts. Wilde, no doubt wisely, refused to go into the box and this distorted image gained some credence. The jury found for Mary Josephine and set damages at one-farthing but Wilde had to bear the entire costs of over £2,000 – as a wit put it, Wilde was charged £2,000 for seducing a girl whose virtue was valued at one farthing!

Wilde now increasingly withdrew from his Dublin activities. The profession stood by him but the labours and exactions of his life had taken their heavy toll. He still saw patients, lectured, wrote, and travelled, and in 1867 produced his brightest and most popular travel book, *Lough Corrib*.[33] But he spent more and more time in his beloved West. He owned a small holding on the wooded peninsula of Illanroe on Lough Fee and now he completed a substantial home at Moytura, near Cong, site of the great pre-historic battle between the Firbolg army of King Eochy, and the forces of the Danaan, which had always fascinated him.[34] His natural son, Henry Wilson, a highly competent ophthalmologist in his own right, increasingly assumed the main duties at St Mark's Hospital. Wilson died unmarried aged 39 in 1877 and left most of his estate of £8,000 to St Mark's and £2,000 to Oscar's brother, Willie, but only £100 to Oscar because of his concern at Oscar's 'Romanist tendencies', and even this was to lapse if Oscar converted – which of course he did, on his death-bed,

---

33 W.R. Wilde, *Lough Corrib, its Shores and Islands* (Dublin, 1867).   34 W.R. Wilde, 'On the Battle of Moytura', *Proceedings of the Royal Irish Academy* 9 (25 June 1866), 546–50; 10 (12 Nov. 1866), 22–24.

but he had spent the money long before.[35] In February 1867 his adored daughter Isola died aged nine, and in November 1871 his two natural daughters, the sisters Emily and Mary, twenty-four and twenty-two, died in a fire following a dance at Drumaconner House in Co. Monaghan. They had been adopted by Wilde's eldest brother, the Revd Ralph Wilde, a somewhat peripatetic clergyman, and so bore the family name. They are buried in St Molina's (Drumsnatt) churchyard nearby off the Smithboro-Monaghan Road: the gravestone says simply,

> In memory of two loving and beloved sisters, Emily Wilde aged 24 years and Mary Wilde aged 22 years who lost their lives by accident in this parish in November 1871
> They were lovely and pleasant in their lives, and in their death they were not divided (2nd Samuel, ch.1, V.23)

Wilde was distraught and his physical and mental deterioration was now obvious. But he finished his Report of the 1871 census on schedule and on St Patrick's Day 1873 he received the Cunningham Gold Medal, the highest award of the Royal Irish Academy. By early 1876 he was increasingly bed-ridden (he had been a life-long asthma sufferer), and in Speranza's words 'he faded away gently before our eyes – still trying to work … and for the last six weeks never left his bed … no pain, thank God, no suffering.'[36] He died on 19 April 1876 at home at 1, Merrion Square, carrying with him to the grave the identities of the mothers of his natural children.

Wilde's will stipulated a private burial at Moytura or, if he died in Dublin, then in the family vault at Mount Jerome. The funeral on the 22nd was far from private: a vast concourse followed the cortège to Mount Jerome led by the president of the Royal Irish Academy, the mace dressed in crape. Over two hundred years before, on Easter Eve 1674, John Graunt, the pioneer vital statistician whom Wilde admired, was buried at St Dunstan's Church in Fleet Street. The diarist, John Aubrey, wrote: 'A great number of ingeniose persons attended Graunt to his grave. Among others, with teares, was that ingeniose great virtuoso Sir William Petty.'[37]

35 J. McA. Curtin, 'Henry Wilson, MD, FRCSI', *Irish Journal of Medical Science* 7th series 2 (Aug. 1969), 369–78. 36 J. Wilde to Sir Thomas Larcom cited in J. Melville, *Mother of Oscar: Life of Jane Francesca Wilde* (London, 1994), p. 128. 37 M. Greenwood, 'Medical Statistics from Graunt to Farr', *Bometrika* 32 (1941–2), 101–27 at p. 108.

Wilde no less than Petty was an 'ingeniose great virtuoso'. Like Ozymandias whose statue lies among those ancient relics which Wilde, revelling in that youth which Oscar would later say was too precious to be wasted on the young, had exuberantly chronicled on his trips as a young bright hopeful doctor forty years before – Wilde deserves Shelley's epitaph from the eponymous sonnet:

'My name is Ozymandias, King of Kings,
look on my works, ye Mighty, and despair.'

POSTSCRIPT

No. 1 Merrion Square bears an oval plaque sculpted by Michael Biggs in Portland stone. It reads:

Sir William Robert Wills Wilde 1815–1876. Aural and ophthalmic surgeon; archaeologist, ethnologist; antiquarian; biographer; statistician; naturalist; topographer; historian; folklorist; lived in this house from 1855–1876.

It was unveiled on the stormy evening of 28 October 1971. Among the speakers were the president of the Royal College of Surgeons (Mr John Paul Lanigan), the president of the Royal Irish Academy (Dr John Raftery), the director of the Economic and Social Research Institute (Dr Roy Geary), the widow of Oscar's younger son (Mrs Vyvyan Holland), and your humble servant. About fifty of us, some in trench-coats against the weather, were huddled around the steps, when a police car disgorged several curious gardaí; and when Dr Raftery started his speech in Irish they moved in thinking that only members of 'an illegal organization' (as the IRA were euphemistically called) would brave the elements *and* be in trench-coats *and* listen to a speech in Irish while being soaked! Roy Geary persuaded them of our impeccable credentials and we disbanded peacefully to enjoy refreshments in the neighbouring hotel.

On the hotel steps I looked back and fancied a tableau – the frail-looking William and the majestic Speranza at their front door. She was articulating her disappointment that we were not that 'illegal organization' whose aims and methods she had once championed in *The Nation*; he was sympathetic about some of the ends, agnostic about others, but opposed to the means, clearly disappointed that we had not stayed to enliven his own table with the informed and witty conversation for which his dinners were justly famous. They turned and together re-entered the house, and I entered the hotel to eat good food and drink good wine with colleagues; activities of which Sir William Robert Wills Wilde would have most heartily approved.

Sir William Wilde and Irish antiquities

MICHAEL RYAN

In *De Profundis,* Oscar Wilde, recalling with pain the forced sale of his possessions, mentions not alone the presentation volumes of almost all the great poets of his day, but especially the 'beautifully bound editions of my father's and mother's works'. On his mother's death, he asserted: 'She and my father had bequeathed me a name they had made noble and honoured not merely in Literature, Art, Archaeology and Science, but in the public history of my own country in its evolution as a nation'[1] – a large claim indeed, but a justified one. His father, William Wilde, has always been viewed as if through a distorting lens. We are tempted to see in William's failings and eccentricities some fateful prefiguration of the Oscar's dreadful fall. We are also partly blinded by the brilliance of the son.

The life of William Wilde was not some mere curtain raiser for a drama that was to follow a quarter-century after his death. He was a man of extraordinary abilities and wide interests, not least of whose qualities was his astonishing appetite for hard work and sustained application. His children's pride in his achievements was justified.[2] A man of prodigious

---

1 O. Wilde, *De Profundis* in *Collins Complete Works of Oscar Wilde*, Centenary Edition (Glasgow, 1999), pp 980–1059, at pp 1003, 1010.   2 His children must have accompanied him on his archaeological work: Oscar Wilde, applying for an archaeological studentship at Oxford in 1879, wrote: 'from my boyhood I have been accustomed, through my father, to visiting and reporting on ancient sites, taking rubbings and measurements and all the technique of *open air* archaeologica – it is of course a subject of intense interest to me.' We know that his son Willie helped him at Glendalough in the 1870s (see T. de Vere White, *The Parents of Oscar Wilde: Sir William and Lady Wilde* (London, 1967), p. 223) and Henry Wilson took an interest in archaeology and published an article on the Lough Gur shield in 1872 (H. Wilson, FRCS, MRIA, 'On a an account of a bronze shield', *Proc. Royal Irish Academy* C 15, (1879) 277–8). It is noteworthy that Wilson was elected a member of the Royal Irish Academy on 8 January 1866. I have been unable to trace his Certificate of nomination to establish who his proposers were but his connection to Wilde, a prominent mem-

energy, interests and talent, much of his work is valuable today to archaeologists and ethnographers. His achievements in medicine, although now
overtaken and eclipsed by modern medical practice, were once honoured
internationally and held their place for a generation or so. His work on
the medical aspects of the decennial Census of Ireland from 1841 to 1871
was stupendous and painstaking. While modern statisticians query some
of his methodology, Wilde created an invaluable asset in orderly and crit-
ically evaluated data and used the work as a platform for notable advances
in demographic, social and medical understanding.

His reputation was rescued from undeserved obscurity by T.G. Wilson's
biography and by de Vere White's authoritative study of Oscar Wilde's parents. An appreciation of his Census work by Froggatt did much to establish
the modern scientific assessment of Wilde the statistician and demographer.[3]

The Ireland into which William Wilde was born in 1817 (at Kilkeevan,
Co. Roscommon) had been changed dramatically by the Act of Union
which was to colour Irish political, social, cultural and economic life for the
following century. The Union called up in Wilde's writings and those of
many like him, an ambivalence which I doubt he ever resolved. Growing
up, Wilde was witness to a very different Ireland from that of more recent
times. The privileged son of a doctor, he was surrounded by the Irish peasantry many of whom were monoglot Irish-speakers.[4] Most of these were
tenants-at-will, living in poverty and vulnerable to famine and associated
infectious diseases. Typhus was endemic and outbreaks of fever in the 1820s
and 30s swept away thousands. The decline in agricultural prices after the
Napoleonic wars was but one of the factors setting the scene for the great
crisis of the Famine of the 1840s. Urban distress was as bad – the cholera
epidemic of 1831–2 in the Liberties of Dublin killed over 20,000 people.
There was a severe economic decline in the 1820s with the collapse of the
textile industry to complicate the problems of overcrowding and disease.

ber of that body and in 1866 probably still the object of some scandalous gossip, can hard-
ly have escaped notice.   3 See T.G. Wilson, *Victorian Doctor being the life of Sir William
Wilde* (London, 1942); T. de Vere White, *The Parents of Oscar Wilde;* P. Froggatt, 'Sir William
Wilde and the 1851 Census of Ireland', *Medical History* 9.4 (October 1965), 302–27 and 'Sir
William Wilde 1815-1876. A Centenary Appreciation: Wilde's Place in Medicine',
Proceedings Royal Irish Academy 77c.10 (1977), 261–78.

Wilde clearly revelled in the customs of the country people amongst whom he grew up in Roscommon and he afterwards devoted a good deal of his writing to recording them, both in the west and in Dublin and Wicklow. In one of his final publications he recalled how he 'schemed out of a Sunday to watch the cake dancers'. He was privileged to see sights which must even then have been remarkable. He recalled a practice at the ancient royal site of Cruachán of driving in all 'the black cattle from the surrounding plains to the great fort on May morning, and bleeding them for the benefit of their health, while crowds of country people, having brought turf for firing, sat around, and cooked the blood mixed with oaten meal, and when they could be procured, onions or *scallions*'.5 He describes faction fights, patterns, and agrarian unrest that amounted to low intensity guerrilla activity. Although he often prettified his accounts when writing about the customs of his youth, making little allusion to rural distress in pre-Famine Ireland, there are some notable descriptions of suffering in the 1840s and 1850s. Some serious re-appraisal of his work in folklore and folklife is long overdue.

His early experiences in Roscommon were an important influence. He was first sent to school in the county, in Elphin. We know little of his time there but he did recall with affection hours spent with Paddy Walsh a local small farmer, flax hackler and not quite a poacher. Paddy was hardly respectable company for a doctor's son. He died when Wilde was just eight years old, and he may have imparted the love of fishing which he kept all his life. He makes Paddy something of a hero in his *Irish Popular Superstitions*, a collection of essays brought together as a book in 1852.6 After Paddy died his son was pressed into the Ribbonmen, a violent agrarian movement. He was killed in an abortive attack on a police barracks at Ballintober and his body exposed on a gibbet mounted on a cart and taken around Roscommon town while other Ribbonmen were flogged at the tails of following vehicles. This act of barbarism caused deep indigna-

4 W.R. Wilde, 'On the Ancient Race of Ireland' in Lady Wilde, *Ancient Legends, Mystic Charms and Superstitions of Ireland. With Sketches of the Irish Past* (London, 1887), ii, p. 342. 5 W.R. Wilde, *Memoir of Gabriel Beranger and his labours in the cause of Irish Art and Antiquities from 1760 to 1780* (Dublin, 1880), p. 77. 6 Wilde's method of working was usually to write a series of articles on a topic, which he then later brought together as a book. Some of his popular writing, his medical biographical work and his textbook on aural surgery follow this pattern.

tion. Wilde's account of the tragedy is one of his most powerful pieces of writing, and he does not spare people of his own class, his summing-up, 'If this was not Connaught, it was Hell',[7] ironically echoing Cromwell. He is sympathetic to the unfortunate youth Michael Walsh, but he also observes that the public display put an end to Ribbonism in Roscommon thereafter. In all his writings Wilde manages to mingle compassion and pragmatism, a kind of strong cultural nationalism and the patriotism of public service with a distinct tinge of monarchism. His indignation at the suffering of the people during and after the Famine is powerful.

At the age of seventeen in 1832, William was sent to Dublin, to Dr Steeven's Hospital, to study surgery under Abraham Colles (1773–1843). After Wilde's first year, the great pandemic of Asiatic cholera reached Ireland. William returned to his family who sent him to his mother's relatives at Cong, Co. Mayo, where he enjoyed an idyllic interlude of country pursuits, recalled with affection in his book on Lough Corrib. During this time he is said to have attended a peddler and his own landlord who were dying of cholera in a house at Kilmaine nearby. Wilde stayed alone with the victims until they died and with the help of a pensioner buried them and fumigated the house before returning to his relatives.

While living at Cong, Wilde made the acquaintance of the enigmatic Father Prendergast.[8] He was a priest who had pretensions to being the last abbot of the great medieval house of Cong. He had in his possession not only a great collection of ancient manuscripts, some of which were cut up for shoe-lining, but also the Cross of Cong, the greatest piece of Irish 12th-century renaissance metalwork. He also held the Shrine of St Patrick's Tooth, which he had impounded from a man who used it to work cures. The Cross came to the collections of the Royal Irish Academy in 1839, the shrine somewhat later through the good offices of the Stokes family. Wilson believed that Fr. Prendergast instilled in Wilde a love of Irish language and culture but there is no compelling evidence that this was so. The assumption has been made also that Wilde was a fluent Irish speaker[9] but as we shall see there is no strong evidence for this and he certainly never claimed to be one.

7 W.R. Wilde, *Irish Popular Superstition* (Shannon, 1972), p. 120. 8 See T.G. Wilson, *Victorian Doctor*, op. cit., pp 6–7, T. de Vere White, *Parents of Oscar Wilde*, op. cit., p. 37. 9 See P. Froggatt, *Sir William Wilde and the 1851 Census*, op. cit., p. 304.

When it was safe to do so, he returned to Dublin to complete his studies, attending the private Park Street medical school in addition to Dr Steeven's Hospital. We know little of Wilde's private life as a student. We do know that he qualified with flying colours in 1837, becoming a licentiate of the Royal College of Surgeons. He had taken the obligatory midwifery training in the Rotunda Hospital and had won the prize in the final examinations. This might suggest steady application and austere habits but we know that later Wilde showed phenomenal powers of concentration and application, so perhaps he crammed for his finals. On qualifying, his health collapsed. It may have been medical concern but it was more likely discretion, that prompted his professors, Dr Graves and Sir Henry Marsh, to obtain for Wilde the appointment as medical attendant on a rich young English invalid, Robert Meiklam; Wilde's son Henry Wilson, mother unknown, was born that year.[10] Mr Meiklam was to cruise in his yacht in the Mediterranean. The voyage was the making of Wilde.

At the age of twenty-three, medically qualified, in poorish health and father of an infant for whose mother he may have had to provide, Wilde set sail with Meiklam. He had never left Ireland and had never been to sea. It was for him a great adventure and a great opportunity, and he seized it with both hands. Reading the account of the voyage, his first major publication, one wonders for whose benefit it was undertaken, his or the patient's. Wilde investigated everything. He wrote a paper on how dolphins suckle their young having dissected a specimen. He pondered the nature of the early inhabitants of Tenerife and of ancient Jerusalem. He described the vaults of mummified ibis at Saqqara (he slept the night in a tomb there surrounded by doubtful characters). He climbed the pyramid of Kephren, an extraordinary feat at the time because it still retained its cladding of polished stone at the top, visited a slave market, noted medical symptoms and took a special interest in ophthalmia (omen for the future). He recorded Hellenistic tombs in Turkey and burial grounds in Jerusalem from which, at some risk, he took skulls for further study.[11] He

10 Henry Wilson followed his father into medicine, became a fellow of the Royal College of Surgeons and assisted Sir William in his practice when his health began to fail in the 1870s. He also shared his father's interest in archaeology. Photographs show that he bore a strong resemblance to both Willie and Oscar who referred to him coyly as a cousin.   11 He was clearly the forerunner of Indiana Jones. Fearing that he would be in difficulties if the sentries at the gates of the city searched his saddlebags and found the bones, he dispersed

opened the tomb of Alonso VI of Portugal unceremoniously to examine the royal remains. The king's head 'was small and the forehead narrow, retracting and unintellectual'. He recorded reams of statistics – of climate and of information useful to invalids travelling in search of health, of steamer schedules to Madeira and tables of mean monthly temperatures. The pragmatist in him warmed to the achievements of Mahomet Ali of Egypt who was attempting to modernize that country after the corruption of Ottoman rule. Everywhere he noted and described 'the ladies': their eyes, their make-up, their dress and manner.[12]

Wilde occasionally speaks of himself as English in the course of the book and we may wonder if he was being somewhat commercial in this choice. The possible interests of an English readership might account for the space he devotes to Sir John Moore's retreat on Corunna and the detail of the battle, which he provides. He also makes numerous references to episodes in Nelson's life. On the other hand, he may have felt more English at the time although he was later more inclined to stress his Irishness. Of mixed ancestry himself, in his very last publication on the ancient races of Ireland, he speaks with enthusiasm of the fusion of Saxon and Celt.[13] The book of his experiences, *Narrative of a Voyage to Madeira, Teneriffe, and along the shore of the Mediterranean* was first published in 1840 and enjoyed a huge success; it was reissued a number of times. The knowledge of Greek and Latin culture, not to mention the Bible, natural history and science generally which simply pours out on every page was quite remarkable.

Wilde's interests took a fresh direction after his return. Together with the distinguished antiquary George Petrie he investigated a site called Lagore, near Dunshaughlin, Co. Meath, which lay on the bed of a drained lake. It was a crannóg or artificial island dwelling of the first millennium AD and their investigations may have been the first scientific examination of a wetland habitation site in Europe. He reported on his work on the bones from the site in the *Transactions of the Royal Irish Academy* in 1840 and in later years was to make much use of his knowledge of ancient animal remains.[14] Petrie, whose task was to record the artefacts, but who was often dilatory, did not play his part and there may have been some coolness between the young surgeon and the eminent anti-

---

them with his whip. **12** See T.G. Wilson, *Victorian Doctor*, op. cit., p. 51. **13** W.R. Wilde, 'On the Ancient Race of Ireland', op. cit., p. 346. **14** Ibid.

quary for a time. This could not have been long-lived as Wilde is known to have kept a portrait of Petrie in his dining room in Merrion Square and he dedicated the first edition of his *Beauties of the Boyne and Blackwater* in 1849, the first of his two great travel books, partly to Petrie.

Wilde decided on a career in optical and aural surgery. He went to London to study at Moorfields Hospital in 1839. Soon he moved on to Austria and there attended at the great General Hospital, the Allgemeines Krankenhaus in Vienna. Wilde's love of statistics shows itself again in the guide he published in 1843, *Austria, its Literary, Scientific and Medical Institutions*, which surveyed, with some criticism, Austria's educational and social system.

It was this statistical bent that led to Wilde becoming Assistant Commissioner for the Census of Ireland for the year 1841. The remarkable report on mortality casts an interesting sidelight on Wilde's antiquarian and linguistic skills. It is quite clear that while he may have had a smattering of Irish, he was not a fluent Irish scholar as has been claimed. In the interests of thoroughness names of diseases were translated from Irish for the police and other enumerators. Wilde relied on intermediaries in his work on the history of disease.[15] Lady Wilde's account of the origins of the fairy-tales in *Ancient Legends of Ireland* (probably in part compiled by her husband or collected for him) suggests that he did the same in his researches in Irish antiquities.[16]

Whatever his competence in Irish, his work in 1841, in which he attempted to combine tables of mortality with a history of disease in Ireland and relate it to the contemporary scene, was remarkable. He carried this to a much higher level of scholarship when he undertook essentially the same

15 Wilde wrote: 'In order to inform myself upon the state of disease in this country at the remotest period to which authentic written records still in existence refer, the Irish MSS., both medical and literary, were examined by a person competent to the task, and such extracts made as afforded a means by which to judge of the condition of disease in this kingdom, in the 14th and 15th centuries.' *Census of Ireland for the year 1841 Report on the Tables of Deaths*, V. A footnote identifies the person as 'Mr Eugene Curry'. Eugene O'Curry (1794–1862) the distinguished Irish scholar and collaborator of Petrie in the great topographical and placenames studies of the Ordnance Survey, became professor of Irish History and Archaeology in the Catholic University of Ireland in 1854.
16 'Many of the Irish legends, superstitions, and ancient charms now collected here were obtained chiefly from oral communications made by the peasantry themselves, either in Irish or in the Irish-English which preserves so much of the expressive idiom of the ancient tongue. These narratives were taken down by competent persons skilled in both languages, and as far as possible in the very words of the narrator; so that much of the primitive simplicity of the style has been retained, while the legends have a peculiar and special value as coming direct from the national heart' in *Ancient Legends*, op. cit., p. xii.

task for the census of 1851 but in a greatly expanded form with, for its time, an exhaustive account of the history of disease in Ireland from the very earliest records. In essence this study is typical of Wilde's approach as an historian of early Ireland. He gives equal weight to the legendary accounts of events and to more sober and plausible histories. In this he is not by any means untypical of his generation. Indeed, the legendary history of Ireland was still taken seriously as factual evidence well into the twentieth century by many, and is enjoying a renewed vogue amongst New Age writers.

Wilde also uses myth and legend in his explanations of monuments. His *Lough Corrib* (first published in 1867) describes the monuments of Mayo and Galway in the vicinity of Cong in the light of the legendary battle of Moytura, identifying and naming sites after characters and episodes in the tale. There is a lack of criticism here surprising in a person who had been exposed to the developments of modern scientific archaeology. It is this avoidance of the uncomfortable uncertainties of archaeological science in favour of the delights and whimsies of traditional lore, that situates Wilde as interpreter much more amongst the antiquaries than amongst the growing band of scientific archaeologists. Despite this, Wilde's descriptions of sites and landscapes are valuable, his writing is vivid and the public reception of his work was remarkable.

Wilde's approach to problems of scholarship in archaeology is perhaps best summed up by the production in 1857–62 of his great catalogue of Irish antiquities. The Royal Irish Academy had since the 1820s been collecting national antiquities by donation, and public subscription. The collection had grown and by the 1850s had become one of the finest of its kind in Europe. It was not a mere accumulation of artefacts; the Academy encouraged scholarship and gradually, with topographical studies and the collection and editing of ancient texts, Irish history and archaeology began to emerge from the state of primitive innocence. George Petrie, John O'Donovan and Eugene O'Curry are names which are indissolubly linked with this process. Petrie was a polymath, an artist and collector of traditional music, greatly beloved. He had a large collection of antiquities, now in the National Museum, but there is no record of them. We rely on a list compiled with the help of his daughter after his death. He seems in retrospect to have been the antithesis of Wilde.

Although the Academy's collection was great, its organisation was in complete disarray and the Council regularly resolved to sort it out. The formation of their collection is described in detail by Mitchell,[17] and the Academy in the 1840s resolved to systematise its museum along scientific lines. Until the early nineteenth century, the prehistoric past was an undifferentiated period of darkness. No reliable empirical method had been devised to penetrate the veil of time and bring some kind of chronological order to the materials which were piling up in collections across Europe. In Denmark, C.J. Thomsen began in 1816–19 to organize the collections of the National Museum by material. He had the insight that the choice of raw materials for the principal tools and weapons might actually reflect a real division in time. His 'Three Ages System' (the ages of stone, bronze and iron) gradually gained acceptance and its broad reliability began to be supported by stratigraphical studies. Thomsen's work was known in Ireland which his brilliant disciple, J.J.A. Worsaae, visited in 1847. He delivered two addresses to the Royal Irish Academy and exchanges between the museums of Dublin and Copenhagen were arranged.[18] The Wildes visited the Copenhagen Museum in 1859, and it is clear from later references by Lady Wilde that the importance of the Copenhagen Museum's intellectual leadership was fully understood by them.[19] The Three Age System was hotly debated in Ireland and Petrie became an early convert to it.

In 1851 Petrie proposed that the Academy's Museum be organized on scientific lines to match the Copenhagen approach, but he was not the man with the drive necessary to complete such a project, nor did the novel doctrine command general agreement. In 1854 new premises were found for the Academy and its museum at 19 Dawson Street, and Wilde threw himself into the task of organizing it with the energy that only he seemed able to find. In August 1857 the British Association for the Advancement of Science was to meet in Dublin. The museum was shaping up but the catalogue project was with Petrie and no progress was made on it. Wilde, seeing that failure to provide a catalogue would be embarrassing, offered in March 1857 to take on the task, which Petrie had neglected. The offer was accepted. He wrote:

17 G.F. Mitchell, 'Antiquities' in T. O'Raifeartaigh (ed.), *The Royal Irish Academy, a bicentennial history 1785–1985* (Dublin, 1985), pp 93–165.   18 Ibid., p. 114.   19 See W.R. Wilde, *Memoir*, op. cit., p. 137.

Some arrangement all will acknowledge would be better than the present state of the museum; such a catalogue, I think it will be admitted, would be better than none, and when it is offered to the Council for the bare cost of the materials, I think they will acknowledge that even as a bare list or invoice of the goods and chattels in the present monster shop of Antiquities, it will be worth what it cost them.[20]

This is the undertaking of a man who less than nine months before had brought a punishing task to a conclusion with his two volumes of the census. He did what he promised and the first volume published in August 1857, 246 finely printed pages and 159 woodcuts, remains one of the cornerstones of Irish archaeology. He worked on Linnaean principles and defined objects by their material with type as a sub-classification. Catalogue descriptions were related to the positions in the exhibition cases in which objects were fixed. There was no overarching numerical system, each series of artifacts beginning with the number 1 – thus we may have many different objects bearing the same W (Wilde) number in the National Collections.[21] Sales were poor and the Academy, ever careful ordered that further volumes would only be published as sales revenue allowed. Two further parts appeared amidst committee infighting in 1861 and 1862 and a fourth fragment was published posthumously in 1916.

Wilde's *Catalogue* brought him an international reputation in antiquities to match and even eclipse his reputation in medicine. The king of Sweden, in 1862, honoured him with the Order of the Polar Star on the recommendation of his friend Von Kraemar, the Governor of Uppsala. He and Speranza had visited Scandinavia in 1859. His medical friends at their dining club jocularly voted to call him Chevalier Wilde and the style given in friendship was later used in gossip to suggest that he was overweening.

It has been said that Wilde's *Catalogue* by ignoring the Three Ages system, marks its author's archaeological work as unscientific. Herity and Eogan imply that Wilde should have known about the new system because

20 In G.F. Mitchell, 'Antiquities', op. cit., p. 119. 21 These created an entirely new art in twentieth-century practice in the National Museum where numbering systems devised by the Academy administration, by Wilde, by William Wakeman, all had to be reconciled with the record. A task surely designed for modern computers.

of Worsaae's visit in 1847.[22] We can thus construct a picture of Wilde as avoiding important theoretical developments in favour of a highly traditionalist approach to the past. I implied such a judgement when this paper was first delivered at the 'Wilde Legacy' conference. I have had the opportunity to reconsider. Wilde chose to work in the way he did because of the enormous haste with which the project was undertaken. It was a perfectly sensible and methodical approach to classification, which would readily provide a platform for refinement and re-analysis. The internal consistency and accuracy of the descriptions are still valuable today. However, Wilde *did* know of, and understand, the system of chronological division into the Ages of Stone, Bronze and Iron but it is clear that he was not fully convinced by it. In his final publication on the ancient races of Ireland he pointed to a number of operational weaknesses in the system and essentially queried whether the chronology could hold good in all places and at all times. He wrote as follows:

> To Northern archaeologists belongs the credit of that theory which divides the ages of man according to the material evidences of the arts of bygone times, as into those of stone, copper, gold, and bronze, and of iron and silver. While I have no doubt that, generally speaking, such was the usual progress of development in those particulars, I deny that this division can, as a rule, be applied to Ireland, where undoubtedly each period overlapped the succeeding, so as to mix one class of implement with another ... I hold it as susceptible of demonstration that man in similar stages of his career all over the world acts alike, so far as is compatible with climate, his wants and the materials that offer to his hand ... Thus wherever man acquires or discovers a new art, he first applies it to continue the fashion of its predecessor, until accident, necessity or ingenuity induces him to modify the reproduction.[23]

That final, and very interesting, paper, which he delivered to the British Association in 1874, was not published until his widow included it in her *Ancient Legends* of 1887. Wilde is clearly torn between the lure of modern

22 See M. Herity and G. Eogan, *Ireland in Prehistory* (London, 1977), pp 10–11. 23 W.R. Wilde, 'On the Ancient Race of Ireland', op. cit., pp 344–5.

theory in archaeology and the critique of it that his own vast experience informed. None of this could resist the tidal force of his belief in the historicity of the legendary accounts of ancient Ireland and much of the paper attempts to reconcile the archaeological evidence with the myths of the Fir Bolg, the Tuatha Dé Danann and the Milesians. The lecture script was not in its first flush of youth when he delivered it in 1874; we know that he had given versions of it to public audiences in Dublin as far back as 1864. We may assume that it represents a distillation of his considered views. As an archaeologist we must accept that in details Wilde was scientific, thorough and well read. On a theoretical level, he was capable of legitimate and well-informed analysis but he found it hard to shake off a mindset formed when he first became exposed to Irish historical scholarship in the 1840s – a mindset reinforced by his innate romanticism.

His *Catalogue* was tied very closely to the arrangement of the museum and Wilde is known to have bitterly resisted any changes to the layout and presentation. A full re-organisation of the collection was carried through under the presidency of Samuel Ferguson but as early as 1880, Lady Wilde bemoaned the disorganization of the museum which broke the connection between the exhibits and the catalogue.[24] She also criticized the Academy's apathy and lack of appreciation for her husband's efforts. She had a point but it is one which forces us to the view that however scientific in detail, Wilde's *Catalogue* was compromised by haste and short-term planning. Linking descriptions to locations in an exhibition which might in time be changed was like building on sand. It is hard to escape the conclusion that Wilde really had conceived of his text as a guide to the exhibitions, albeit an extensive and detailed one.

Although he loved the Academy and laboured long for it he was not fully accepted by it. Its highest honour, the Cunningham Medal, was first suggested for him in 1861. However, a series of what the official historian calls 'indecisive meetings chiefly noted for significant absences'[25] ensued and he was finally voted the medal by a meeting with a bare quorum. Wilde promptly rejected it though some of his friends thought that he had been too hasty, one of them saying, 'his nature is too impulsive'. He was their outstanding member but the presidency never came his way.

24 W.R. Wilde, *Memoir*, op. cit., p. 139. 25 G.F. Mitchell, 'Antiquities', op. cit., p. 122.

Mitchell concluded that they thought that he was not quite a gentle-man.[26] Perhaps they were wary of being associated with a life that was less than conventional. In 1871, five years after he had been rocked by scandal, the Academy voted him the medal warmly and he accepted it.

Wilde's life from about 1860 until his death was filled with achievement and triumph, tragedy and farce. He was knighted in 1864, loaded with honours of all kinds but the decade saw the death of his three daughters – Isola in 1867 and his two illegitimate daughters, Mary and Emily in a fire in 1871. The extraordinary relationship with Mary Travers which led to the sensational libel trail of 1864 must have exacted a heavy physical toll on Wilde and his family, but there is no evidence to suggest that Sir William's work rate declined or that his enthusiasms were impaired. He continued to publish in all his areas of interest. His *Lough Corrib* appeared three years after the trial but he did increasingly escape to Moytura, his house near Cong, when he could. He worked hard to restore the monuments of the area and campaigned vigorously to protect sites elsewhere, in Roscommon for example in 1870. It was about this time that he began to collect for posterity the antiquarian drawings of Gabriel Beranger and publish, first in serial form, the memoir of the artist's life. This contains much information about Wilde and about his own work on monuments as well as a eulogy by Lady Wilde. It also contains many valuable first-hand descriptions of traditions, events and monuments. Up to a few months before he died, he was engaged with his son Willie to restore and describe the ruins of Glendalough monastery. The account appears in the memoir. That final work in the field reminds us that Wilde was not just an investigator, he was one of the great pioneers of conservation of ancient monuments and the protection and recording of archaeological records. Our debt to him is very deep.

26 Ibid.

OSCAR WILDE

Eternal loss and sadness: the fairy tales of Oscar Wilde

ROBERT DUNBAR

When he grew tired of playing he would keep us quiet by telling us fairy stories, or tales of adventure, of which he had a never-ending supply. He was a great admirer of Jules Verne and Stevenson, and of Kipling in his more imaginative vein. The last present he gave me was *The Jungle Book*; he had already given me *Treasure Island* and Jules Verne's *Five Weeks in a Balloon*, which were the first books I read through entirely by myself. He told us all his own written fairy stories suitably adapted for our young minds, and a great many others as well. There was one about the fairies who lived in the great bottles of coloured water that chemists used to put in their windows, with lights behind them that made them take on all kinds of different shapes. The fairies came down from their bottles at night and stayed and danced and made pills in the empty shop. Cyril once asked him why he had tears in his eyes when he told us the story of 'The Selfish Giant', and he replied that really beautiful things always made him cry.[1]

Historians of children's literature tend to view the nineteenth century, particularly its second half, as a golden age. Undoubtedly, it is from this period that there date most of what would generally be seen as the 'classics' of the genre, though revisionary notions of canonicity are beginning to apply here as much as in other literary areas. Still, it was the era of, among others, Kingsley's *The Water Babies*, Carroll's *Alice* books, MacDonald's *At the Back of the North Wind*, Lear's limericks, Hughes' *Tom Brown's Schooldays*, Stevenson's *Treasure Island*, Marryat's *The Children of the New Forest*, Sewell's *Black Beauty*, Kipling's *Jungle Books* and, as the century ended,

[1] V. Holland, *Son of Oscar Wilde* (London, 1957), p. 45.

Nesbit's *The Story of The Treasure Seekers*. Some at least of these were part of Wilde's reading and, subsequently, his children's. But what Vyvyan Holland refers to as his father's 'own written stories', the nine works that comprise his collections *The Happy Prince and Other Stories* (1888) and *A House of Pomegranates* (1891) have their locus in a more specialised development in Victorian writing for the young, which I want to trace briefly and chronologically, and which may be seen as starting with the first translations, in 1823 and 1826, of what we now refer to as *Grimms' Fairy Tales*. I should say in passing that the phrase 'Victorian writing for the young' is, as is widely recognised, extremely problematic and famously so in consideration of the possible audience, or audiences, for Wilde's stories. Declan Kiberd, in a meticulously punctuated sentence in the most recent comment on this topic in his *Irish Classics* writes: 'Wilde's fairy tales are intended, perhaps mainly, for adults – but for children too.'[2] In the earliest criticism, an anonymous review in *The Athenaeum* of September 1888, we read:

> There is a piquant touch of contemporary satire which differentiates Mr Wilde from the teller of pure fairy tales; but it is so delicately introduced that the illusion is not destroyed and a child would delight in the tales without being worried or troubled by their application, while children of larger growth will enjoy them and profit by them.[3]

A month later, Alexander Galt Ross was writing in the *Saturday Review*: 'Mr Oscar Wilde, no doubt for excellent reasons, has chosen to present his fables in the form of fairy tales to a public which ... will assuredly not be composed of children.'[4] An unsigned review of *A House of Pomegranates* in the *Pall Mall Gazette* of 1891 begins: 'Is *A House of Pomegranates* intended for a child's book? We confess that we do not exactly know', though a later sentence would seem to settle the reviewer's uncertainties: 'Children may be very much attached to bric-á-brac (though of this we have our doubts), but the more natural among them

---

2 D. Kiberd, *Irish Classics* (London, 2000), p. 326. 3 Unsigned notice, in K. Beckson (ed.), *Oscar Wilde: The Critical Heritage* (London, 1970), p. 60. 4 A.G. Ross, *Saturday Review*, 20 October 1888 in *Critical Heritage*, op. cit., p. 61.

would certainly prefer Hansel and Gretel's sugar-house to any amount of Mr Wilde's "rich tapestries" and "velvet canopies".'[5] It was this review which in turn prompted Wilde's celebrated riposte in a letter to the *Gazette*. 'Now in building this *House of Pomegranates* I had as much intention of pleasing the British child as I had of pleasing the British public.'[6] And as we have seen in my opening quotation from Vyvyan Holland, Wilde's telling of the stories to his own children involved some measure of 'suitable adaptation' for their 'young minds'.

These early conflicting views of intended readership continue to be echoed in most later examinations of Wilde's stories, though in the context of the genre of fairy tales and of the Victorian period they cannot be seen as uniquely Wildean problems. Nor are they matters of exclusively literary concern, since they demand an awareness of evolving notions of what are nowadays often referred to as 'constructions' of childhood, adolescence and adulthood. 'Children's literature' in the Victorian era was not the strongly differentiated genre which it was later to become: very few of the Victorian writers whom I shall be mentioning as Wilde's precursors wrote exclusively for children, though they may all have written at least one children's book and, of course, they may all have written in their adult books about childhood. The most succinct summary of the situation is in U.C. Knoepflmacher's *Ventures into Childland* where he comments: 'The traffic between adult and child was, in effect, an intrinsic part of all the authorial identities the Victorians concocted in their public efforts to make sense of their world.'[7] As for the world of fairy tale, centuries had passed between their oral origins and their first appearance in written form in English, initially as versions from the French, in the early eighteenth century. Almost from the outset, arguments ensued as to whether they were appropriate reading material for children, the controversy shifting between views of their total undesirability, views of their usefulness as vehicles of didactic instruction and views of their respectability – by no means totally unchallenged – as sources of imaginative awe, wonder and curiosity.

But to return to the 1820s: the first translations of Grimm had had a strong impact. True, there had been earlier collections of fairy tales for

---

5 *Critical Heritage*, op. cit., p. 113.   6 Ibid., p. 13.   7 U.C. Knoepflmacher, *Ventures into Childland: Victorians, Fairy Tales, and Femininity* (Chicago and London, 1998), p. xv.

children, many of them having to compete for a readership and acceptance in a time dominated by exclusive notions of the useful and the purposeful in children's books: but with the arrival of the Grimm stories the literary future of the fantasy and fairy tale for children was assured and an impetus provided for writers to invent their own 'fairy' narratives. In the context of contemporary developments in Ireland, the same decade which produced the Grimms saw also the publication of the two volumes of T. Crofton Croker's *Fairy Legends and Traditions of the South of Ireland* (1825) which, while not specifically perceived as being for a child readership, provided landscapes, both geographical and of the mind, which later Irish children's writers – even today's – were to plunder enthusiastically. In his book *The Thief of Reason: Oscar Wilde and Modern Ireland,* Richard Pine refers to what he sees as 'the neglect of Irish folklore as an influence on Wilde's own tales', going on to advance as a first reason for this 'neglect' that it is too easy to make comparisons between his work and that of the Brothers Grimm and Hans Christian Andersen.[8] But undeterred by this admonition and while acknowledging Pine's fascinating demonstration of the link between some of Lady Wilde's *Ancient Legends of Ireland* and her son's stories and while acknowledging the scholarly work of others who have focused on similar links, it is impossible to leave Andersen, in particular, completely out of the frame of Wilde's influences. His stories had first begun to appear in English translation in 1846 and if we require a relevant proof of their speedy assimilation and significance we can find it in the stories in Frances Browne's *Granny's Wonderful Chair,* first published in 1856, only ten years on. This book is usually mentioned in a footnote to histories of (English) children's literature in accounts of the Victorian popularity of literary fairy tales and inevitably in the same paragraph which mentions the contemporary translations of Andersen's stories – fairly enough, perhaps, given that in her final paragraph Browne hails Andersen as 'one whose tales of the fairies are so good that they must have been heard from themselves'.[9] But what is hardly ever remembered is that Browne was born in 1816 in a small village in Donegal, where she spent the first thirty-six years of her life before moving to London. 'Once upon a time,' begins the story called 'The Story of Merrymind' 'there

8 R. Pine, *The Thief of Reason: Oscar Wilde and Modern Ireland* (New York, 1995), p. 180.
9 F. Browne, *Granny's Wonderful Chair* (London, 1963), p. 150.

lived in the north country a certain poor man and his wife, who had two cornfields, three cows, five sheep and thirteen children',[10] a setting of some local veracity, one suspects. The paired characterization which Browne favours so much – the brothers Scrub and Spare, the brothers Clutch and Kind, the brothers Sour and Civil – affords a study in the dualities typical of colonized society, with all of them competing for power and expression. Similarly, her elemental and stylized settings, such as the cottage, the forest and the big house, while found in many folk and fairy tales, have a particular resonance when seen in an Irish context. There is much here which, some thirty years later, will resurface, with variations, in Wilde.

As for Andersen, as recent biographies such as Alison Prince's and Jackie Wullschlager's have made clear, the double-layered structures of his stories serve as screens behind which he masks his own complexities and vulnerabilities, often overlaid by a savage black humour which does not totally eradicate their occasional penchant for sentimentality; it is the ongoing dialectic between a series of vivid oppositions which dominates his work and, the evidence suggests, his life also; there are enigmas, contradictions and ambiguities in both.[11] If, at one moment, Andersen seems to endorse the notion of personal triumph over adversity, at another he proposes domains of disappointed fortunes, disillusioned romance and apparently pointless sacrifice. These were themes with which the Wilde of the two volumes of fairy stories, where dying for love is a recurring motif, would become familiar.

He would doubtlessly have been familiar also with his friend John Ruskin's single entry into the world of literary fairy tale in the form of *The King of the Golden River*, first published in 1851. But there are more ironies and contradictions here: for while Ruskin was later to declare against what he called 'moral fairy tales' for children,[12] his own effort in the genre overtly preaches the virtue of generosity and self-abnegation. Switch to the closing words of Wilde's 'The Devoted Friend':

> 'I'm afraid you don't quite see the moral of the story,' remarked the Linnet.

10 Ibid., p. 127. 11 See A. Prince, *Hans Christian Andersen: The Fan Dancer* (London, 1998) and J. Wullschlager, *Hans Christian Andersen: The Life of a Storyteller* (London, 2000). 12 J. Ruskin, 'Fairy Stories' (1868) in Robert L. Wolff (ed.), *Masterworks of Children's Literature, 1837–1900* (New York, 1985), p. 167.

'The what?' screamed the Water-Rat.

'The moral.'

'Do you mean to say that the story has a moral?'

'Certainly,' said the Linnet.

'Well, really,' said the Water-Rat, in a very angry manner, 'I think you should have told me that before you began. If you had done so, I certainly would not have listened to you; in fact, I should have said 'Pooh' like the critic.'

[He disappeared into his hole] ...

'And how do you like the Water-Rat?' asked the Duck, who came paddling up some minutes afterwards...

'I am rather afraid that I have annoyed him,' answered the Linnet. 'The fact is that I told him a story with a moral.'

'Ah! That is always a very dangerous thing to do,' said the Duck.

Last line, no inverted commas: *And I quite agree with her.*[13]

The tongue-in-cheek Wildean ironies which abound in a passage such as this are prefigured in another literary fairy tale, Thackeray's parodic and satirical *The Rose and the Ring,* first appearing in 1855. Here, when the Fairy Blackstick decides to abandon her practice of bestowing gifts on children at birth, she says to Prince Giglio, the story's hero, 'My poor child, the best thing I can send you is a little misfortune,' before treating the heroine, the Princess Rosalba, in the same way.[14] Since, however, the work is deliberately subtitled 'A Fire-side Pantomime', we can justifiably expect that true love will ultimately conquer, though not before we are exposed to a sequence of incongruities, including the essential one where-by the fairy's donation of 'a little misfortune' turns out to be as valuable for Giglio and Rosalba as the kingdoms they eventually inherit. In its blended presentation of childhood innocence and adult knowingness, *The Rose and the Ring* can simultaneously incorporate the mixed blessings of hindsight and anticipation: the same fusion will typify much of the spirit of Wilde's nine tales, likewise controlled by irony and wishfulness

---

13 O. Wilde, 'The Devoted Friend' in *Collins Complete Works of Oscar Wilde,* Centenary edition (Glasgow, 1999), pp 286-93 at p. 293.   14 W.M. Thackeray, 'The Rose and the Ring; or History of Prince Giglio and Prince Bulbo' (1885) in *Masterworks of Children's Literature,* op. cit., p. 73.

and, albeit with different nuances, informed by a psychological under-standing of the process of maturation.

With the appearance in 1863 of Kingsley's *The Water Babies*, subtitled 'A Fairy Tale for a Land Baby', the fairy tale of mid-Victorian England under-goes a key transformation, allowing itself to question its own nature and purpose. Rambling, diffuse and indeed chaotic as Kingsley's book is, in its disorder is mirrored the disorder and moral chaos of the society which it so searingly assaults. This is an angry fairy tale, striking out against cruelty and social injustice, fuelled by its author's Christian Socialist convictions and given expression in a linguistic ebullience which is at times dizzying. In matters of form, Wilde's stories are exemplars of self-control, by contrast with Kingsley's circumnavigations: but what they share, particularly in such works as 'The Happy Prince' and 'The Young King', is a humane concern with the evils of the underbelly of Victorian complacency and self-content. Jack Zipes, in his essay 'The Flowering of the Fairy Tale in Victorian England', makes the point that from the 1850s onwards, 'various English writers began to explore the potential of the fairy tale as a form of literary communication that might convey both individual and social protest and personal conceptions of alternative, if not utopian worlds' and goes on to say that 'to write a fairy tale was considered by many writers a social symbolical act that could have implications for the education of chil-dren and the future of society.'[15] While he mentions no names, it seems rea-sonable to suggest that this particular exploration could be seen as starting with Kingsley and taking us eventually to Wilde. Jerusha McCormack, in her essay 'Wilde's fiction(s)', asserts: 'It is from the margins of society, from the perspective of the poor, the colonised, the disreputable and dispos-sessed, that the stories must be read.'[16]

There is one final major name to be mentioned within this grouping of writers sharing what, as already quoted, Zipes designates 'conceptions of alternative, if not utopian worlds.' This is George MacDonald, friend of Carroll and Kingsley, and certainly as tuned as the latter to matters of social inequality and deprivation. In his best known children's fantasy, *At*

15 J. Zipes, 'The Flowering of the Fairy Tale in Victorian England', *When Dreams Came True: Classical Fairy Tales and Their Tradition* (New York and London, 1999), p. 118. 16 J. McCormack, 'Wilde's Fiction(s)' in P. Raby (ed.), *The Cambridge Companion to Oscar Wilde* (Cambridge, 1998), p. 102.

the Back of the North Wind, published in book form in 1871, Diamond, the boy hero, with his extensive store of innate goodness is a Christ-like child, whose suffering is represented as a learning process: he is endowed with a radical innocence and an education, via some form of purgatorial experience, is necessary if he is to come to understand some of the manifestations of goodness in the world in which he has found himself: this, paradoxically, is how he will ultimately cope with the travails of his existence. In much of MacDonald's writing, within the contours of the oldest fairy tales, there is the repeated yearning note for a desired better world which quest stories traditionally embody: it is a blend which, sad endings and all, was to appeal to Wilde. In his essay on Wilde in *Irish Classics*, Kiberd indicates how the 'Christ-like figures of [Wilde's] children's stories embrace poverty, shame and social ostracism', and intriguingly links 'The Selfish Giant' with Pearse's *Iosagán*, 'with its idea of a Christ child bearing redemptive messages to a fallen adult world'.[17]

Stylistically, also, the discordant modes of MacDonald's prose will find an echo in Wilde's collections. An excerpt such as the following from his *Phantastes*, subtitled 'A Faerie Romance for Men and Women', describing the decor of the library of a fairy palace, exemplifies his ornate bejewelled manner:

> All round the walls in front of the books ran galleries in rows, communicating by stairs. These galleries were built of all kinds of coloured stones; all sorts of marble and granite, with porphyry, jasper, lapis lazuli, agate and various others, were ranged in a wonderful melody of successive colours. Although the material, then, of which the galleries and stars were built, rendered necessary a certain degree of massiveness in the construction, yet such was the size of the place, that they seemed to run along the wall, like cords. Over some parts of the library descended curtains of silk of various dyes...[18]

And so on. The 'wonderful melody of successive colours' here clearly includes a Wildean purple and has much relevance to a consideration of a further Jerusha McCormack observation that 'the only interest of the

17 D. Kiberd, *Irish Classics*, op. cit., p. 326.   18 G. MacDonald, 'Phantastes' (1858) in C.N. Manlove, *Modern Fantasy: Five Studies* (Cambridge, 1975), p. 92.

[Wilde] tale is an engagement of language with itself as a kind of pure verbal declaration'.[19] A review of Wilde's *Intentions*, published in *The Speaker* magazine in 1891, comments how he is 'conscious of the charm of graceful echoes and is always original in his quotations'.[20] I trust the same could be said of all of us. Certainly, with the MacDonald library still in mind, it is with some sense of *déjà vu* that we come in 'The Young King' to a paragraph describing the 'dimly-lit room' in which the prince anticipates his coronation:

> A large press, inlaid with agate and lapis lazuli, filled one corner, and facing the window stood a curiously wrought cabinet with lacquer panels of powdered and mosaiced gold, on which were placed some delicate goblets of Venetian glass, and a cup of dark-veined onyx. Pale poppies were broidered on the silk coverlet of the bed, as though they had fallen from the tired hands of sleep ...[21]

But co-existing with this 'over-sweetness' in MacDonald, as C.S. Lewis described it,[22] there is a bleak undertow of sobriety, an antidote to the coruscating embellishment: it is as if there are dualities which can never be quite balanced between worlds of mystery and imagination and places dominated by 'the weariness, the fever and the fret, /Here, where men sit and hear each other groan.' 'Keats is the greatest of them,' Ellmann quotes Wilde as having said.[23] 'Far away, in an orchard,' we read in 'The Young King', 'a nightingale was singing.' In his own essay on the fairy tale, 'The Fantastic Imagination', published in 1893, MacDonald writes of the 'broken music' of fairy tale that goes 'for a firefly that now flashes, now is dark, but may flash again'.[24] It is an image which simultaneously bears on how we read MacDonald (and Wilde) and reminds us of how the fluctuating 'sweetness' and 'sobriety' in their choice of language reflects the dualities in their respective imaginations.

As I was trying to sort out these basic ideas on Wilde's fairy tales, news came from America of the death of Robert Cormier, generally regarded as

---

19 J. McCormack, 'Wilde's Fiction(s)', op. cit., p. 103.   20 [Arthur Symons] Unsigned review, *The Speaker*, 4 July 1891 in *Critical Heritage*, op. cit., p. 96.   21 O. Wilde, 'The Young King' in *Complete Works*, op. cit., pp 213–22 at p. 215.   22 C.S. Lewis, *George MacDonald: An Anthology* (London, 1946), p. 14.   23 R. Ellmann, *Oscar Wilde* (London, 1987), p. 252.   24 Quoted in W. Reaper, *George McDonald* (Tring, 1987), p. 315.

one of the most important of twentieth-century writers for young adults. In what I consider his most striking novel, *Fade*, there is a moment when its young teenage hero, Paul Moreaux, first visits the home of a school friend, Emerson Winslow. On Emerson's phonograph is a record by Bunny Berigan. Cormier describes Paul's reaction to the music as follows: 'I heard for the first time the tortured beauty of Bunny Berigan's trumpet, golden notes bruised with sadness, rising and falling ... I sensed that it was moving towards a climax, as if the trumpeter were building an invisible structure in the air, rising, rising towards a pinnacle that was both triumphant and blazing with eternal loss and sadness.'[25] I think the Wilde of the fairy tales – and much else besides – would have known what young Paul meant.

25 R. Cormier, *Fade* (London, 1988), p. 96.

Oscar Wilde's fairy tales
on stage in 2001

MARY ELIZABETH BURKE-KENNEDY

The House of Pomegranates, Oscar Wilde's collection of fairy tales, consists of nine stories. Unlike other European fairy tales, which end happily ever after, Wilde's stories end on the note of death. The heroes of his stories find themselves trapped by vanity, pride, greed and arrogance. They achieve redemption at great cost and through suffering. While the folk tales collected by the Brothers Grimm and Italo Calvino come from ancient oral traditions, and have been shaped by generations of storytellers, Wilde's stories are the product of a single imagination and his voice comes through distinctly.

In the older stories, apart from the celebration of weddings, there is no evidence of any religious orthodoxy. The good deeds of the hero are rewarded, generally by his getting the girl he loves, and half her father's kingdom. Wilde's fairy land is emphatically Christian. People commit sins, are punished and realise the error of their ways. The reward for doing good is to be sent to Heaven. These are explicitly moral tales with very strong messages. But for all that, Wilde's stories luxuriate in exotic imagery and sensory detail.

The invitation to adapt these stories for the stage, for an audience of twenty-first century children, was, at first, daunting. The first part of the process involved elimination.

'The Nightingale and the Rose', 'The Birthday of the Infanta' and 'The Devoted Friend' deplore the vanity and mendacity of the privileged. The Nightingale, the Dwarf and Little Hans all offer up their lives in the service of ungrateful masters. These are dark, angry stories. They provoke a response of outrage in the reader, but not the kind of theatrical uplift I was looking for, for our audience.

'The Remarkable Rocket' is a sophisticated satire on self-importance, and the language is close to the language of Wilde's plays, but it has no scope for audience identification.

'The Fisherman and his Soul', while it is given the trappings of a fairy tale, with a mermaid lover, a witch and a series of trials for the hero, is ultimately a complicated rumination on religion and spirituality. 'The Young King' is a parable, peopled with allegorical figures. The hero is a cipher. With no relationships, he is just a soul awaiting transfiguration.

The remaining stories are 'The Star-Child', 'The Happy Prince' and 'The Selfish Giant'. As with the other stories, the language has the archaic resonance of the King James Bible, the imagery is lush with opulent textures and colours and the themes of selfishness, atonement and redemption are common to the three tales. What makes them appealing to children is partly their playful use of animals and birds as central characters in the action. But what has made them over the years the most accessible of the stories of this collection is the huge emotional impact they carry.

The magic of the relationship between the Prince and the Swallow transcends the danger of 'The Happy Prince' becoming a tract about the gulf between the rich and the poor. The same magic is at work in 'The Selfish Giant', in the dazzling transparency of the writing, and the child-like innocence of the Giant. 'The Star-Child' is probably the most conventional fairy story in the collection, but it speaks powerfully to everyone who has had a falling-out with his or her parents.

The challenge in presenting these fairy tales on the stage was twofold. First, how could we find a range of images to cover the scale of those contained in the stories? How could we transport the audience from a snow-bound forest, to the Prince's city with its great cathedral, to the Nile with its yellow lions, and back to the Giant's garden, with children sitting in every peach tree? How could we people the stage with woodcutters, magicians, lepers, courtiers, camels, beggars, angels, red ibises, the Sphinx, a giant and a menagerie of animals? Second, how could we ensure that we engaged the concentration of the Playstation generation for an hour and a half? The answer to both problems was to let Oscar Wilde take care of it.

We chose a theatrical form of storytelling, which brought the focus directly on to Wilde's narrative. The settings were non-naturalistic rather than literal. Suspended blue and white silk became icy mountains, billowing snow-drifts and the mountain torrent. Gathering the white silk around their shoulders, actors became the white marble angels on the cathedral spire. Thus the staging was suggestive, allowing the audience to engage with the narrative and imagine for themselves. In this way, the power of Oscar Wilde's language was exploited to the full.

While the three stories we selected are connected thematically and stylistically, they have no dramatic connection or unity. The objective of the adaptation was to supply this. The structure of the play includes a framing device, a play about a group of animals, stranded in the forest during a blizzard. To pass the night and to distract themselves from their dire situation, they tell stories and they play the roles in the stories that are appropriate to their animal characters. The Hare, The Linnet and The Wolf come directly from the tales themselves. The Bear, The Deer, The Falcon and The Vixen have been added. The play poses the questions, "Will the animals and birds survive the night or will they freeze to death? Will they turn on each other?" The telling of the stories helps to keep their predatory instincts at bay and inspires them for their future.

This device gives the unity of time and place that the dramatisation requires. From this particular place in the forest, on this particular night, the forest creatures let their imaginations take flight. So too do the imaginations of the audience, spurred on by Oscar Wilde's poetic narrative.

The director of the production, Bairbre Ní Chaoimh, wanted to explore the possibilities of playing with scale in this production. Her idea for the staging of 'The Selfish Giant' was that rather than putting an actor into a gigantic costume, we should find a way of reducing the size of the actors playing the children. So the children were played by beautifully crafted puppets, hand-held and voiced by the actors. The Giant retained his humanity and was saved from becoming a grotesque. The visions that the Happy Prince has of his city were played by shadow-puppets. The Dressmaker and her son, the Poet and the Match-girl, all appear on screens, as the Prince describes their tribulations to the Swallow. The animals, whose situation provides the engine of the play, were represented by hand-held head masks, while the world of the play was presented on stage in its entirety, by an illuminated model. This switching of the focus of scale provided many perspectives for the audience to engage with the play. It also captured theatrically the duality of Wilde's stories, where animate and inanimate creatures converse and relate.

The unequivocal moral tone of the stories posed no problem to an audience of children. Children have a strong sense of justice. They can recognise cruelty, vanity and selfishness when they see them. They can empathize with victims and they understand the relief of forgiveness. For children, the suspension of disbelief is automatic, so there is no problem in the concept of a swallow falling in love with a reed, or a hare talking to a human boy, or a giant playing with a group of children. The challenge for them is the nature of theatre itself. They have to realize that the performance is not animated, not an interactive game, but live. It is happening for them, there and then, and they must keep up. It is a measure of the continuing power of Oscar Wilde's fairy tales, that children in the theatre in the twenty-first century sit spellbound and rapt by his magic.

Panel discussion:
Wilde in the theatre

MARINA CARR, THOMAS KILROY,
PATRICK MASON, MICHAEL COLGAN, CHAIRMAN

MICHAEL COLGAN: It's interesting to be here as chair because I have worked with directors and writers for the most of my life. It's a profession that is given to disobedience at best (they never listen to what I say), so today I am going to get my revenge! In the theatre, I have enjoyed working with each member of the panel enormously. I regard them as friends and people I admire not only for their talents but, also, for their integrity. Therefore, what I am hoping to get today is a discussion that we might have at a dinner party in one of our houses.

Recently, the *Irish Times* printed an article, in many ways a 'dinner party article', about reading the future. It included a list of those who in the writer's opinion would be seen as classics in the future; and, with great respect to Tom Kilroy and no disrespect to Marina Carr, I thought it was the most preposterous list I came across in my entire life. I began to wonder if Oscar Wilde would have made it on to such a list if it had been made 100 years ago, and that led me on a journey of thinking about greatness. We are all here, after all, to celebrate the greatness, and the legacy, of Oscar Wilde.

D.H. Lawrence once said that we are all susceptible to what's expected of us, and maybe it's expected of everybody here to say that Oscar Wilde really was great. And maybe he wasn't. But maybe he was. On my way here, I passed by the house he lived in, in Merrion Square, and the plaque read, 'Oscar Wilde, Poet, Dramatist and Wit', and I noticed that the descriptions weren't in alphabetical order. 'Dramatist' didn't get top billing, but would all of us be here because of his poetry? Would all of us be here because of his wit?

I think it is very difficult to work out what is great in the theatre or in writing. Is something great because people in the theatre say it's great? Or because academics say it's great? Or because producers decide to produce this work? Or because people come to it in their droves? And is Oscar a great dramatist? I don't know the answer, but I think that greatness might be something to do with the ability to survive scrutiny and, in some way, to weather interpretation. I am at the moment making nineteen films of the work of Samuel Beckett and I know there is going to be controversy about whether we should turn his plays into films. And these people, who I know are going to attack me for doing it, are trying to protect Beckett, and I somehow feel that he doesn't need that protection. I feel that Beckett can survive, and I feel that when we talk about greatness in the theatre or greatness in the dramatist we are talking about the ability to survive.

When I'm sitting in the Gate Theatre in Parnell Square on a wet Tuesday working on what I'm going to do, there is no question that the safe option of all the dramatists is Oscar Wilde. In the time I've been at the Gate I have produced *Salomé*, a version of *Dorian Gray, The Importance of Being Earnest*, directed by Patrick Mason, *Lady Windermere's Fan*, and even repeated myself by doing two versions of *An Ideal Husband*. My first introduction to Wilde was in a great production of *A Woman of No Importance* directed by Patrick when we first worked together. And I find that there is no doubt that the Gate theatre has absolutely and without any question survived and avoided going in to liquidation because of Oscar Wilde; not just during my tenure, seventeen years, but in Hilton Edwards' and Micheál MacLiammóir's time. He is the most popular dramatist there is in Ireland today. But what I am hoping will come out of this discussion, is not an acceptance of Oscar as the great dramatist but a challenge to that. Is he great? When I asked Stephen Berkoff to direct *Salomé*, he remarked that it was a great play, but the other plays were just boulevard comedies. The best thing for us to do is to ask each of our panel, Marina, Tom and Patrick to say something about this. More particularly, I would like them to say something about how Oscar has affected their own careers or their own visions of theatre.

MARINA CARR: I don't think there is any question whether he is great or not. In my mind, anyway, he is great, and he continues to be greater the more I grow up. To speak about how much he has influenced me, unfortunately, I have to say, 'not enough', but I hope to remedy that. One of the problems of talking about Oscar Wilde is that he says everything about himself best, so you end up quoting him all the time. So, at the risk of insulting the general public (which he enjoyed doing), I'll begin with a quote from the essay 'The Decay of Lying'. He is talking about theatre.

> The characters in these plays talk on the stage exactly as they would talk off it; they have neither aspirations not aspirates; they are taken directly from life and reproduce its vulgarity down to the smallest detail; they present the gait, manner, costume and accent of real people, they would pass unnoticed in a third-class railway carriage. And yet how wearisome the plays are! They do not succeed in producing even that impression of reality at which they aim, and which is their only reason for existing. As a method, realism is a complete failure.[1]

He wrote this over 100 years ago, and it is still true today. He goes on to say that ours is certainly the dullest and most prosaic century possible. 'Art', says Wilde, closing the argument, 'never expresses anything but itself'.[2]

And that leads me to Wilde himself: Wilde was a walking work of art. Anyone who has read the biographies will realize that. To say that appearance was important to him is an understatement: the green carnation, the Egyptian gold cigarettes. And one cannot forget that he was ordering gloves and neckties during the tragedy of incarceration. There is a sense that the first half of his life was a comedy and the second half a tragedy – albeit in fifty-five acts.

The joy of reading Wilde and reading about Wilde is that there are so many Wildes. He spoke of the mask in 'The Decay of Lying'. The most interesting thing about people is the mask that every one wears, and not the reality that hides behind the mask. The plays are full of masks and the plays are, among other things, also about Wilde's several selves, albeit strained through the muslin of art. They are imagined lives, which he pur-

1 O. Wilde, 'The Decay of Lying' in *Collins Complete works of Oscar Wilde*, Centenary edition (Glasgow, 1999), pp 1071–92 at pp 1079–80.   2 Ibid., p. 1087.

sued all his life in the quest for self-realisation, a quest which was of paramount importance and cost him greatly. And, reading the work and reading Ellmann and other surrounding material, you get a sense of how brave he was. And of how hard it was to hold equilibrium knowing doom was pending. There is the famous story of the palmist Cherio reading his palm when he is thirty-eight. Cherio tells him he is going to destroy himself. Wilde asks when, and Cherio says 'in around your fortieth year'. And though this prophecy is made known to him, Wilde goes and embraces it. There are other things that are extraordinary when you read the biography beside the work. He wrote *The Importance of Being Earnest* just as the sky was about to fall in during that last summer before the proceedings that led to the terrible trial and imprisonment. You've got all that glitter and gaiety and wit and then, and this is the extraordinary thing about Wilde, the undertow Wilde, the Greek tragic Wilde, the double-first Oxford graduate, the Wilde who wrote *De Profundis, Salomé, The Ballad of Reading Gaol* and those beautiful letters and conversations which his friends and acquaintances had the good sense to record.

The whole question mark over the greatness of Wilde hinges on the fact that the life and the work are so inseparable, that he did make out of his life a work of art, a beautiful pristine thing early on and then a terrible Greek tragedy towards the last seven or eight years. The Happy Prince says to the Swallow: 'There is no Mystery so great as Misery'.[3] And, even in his misery, Wilde did find an articulation of that mystery in the late work and in some of the letters. I quote: 'Life held to my lips, a full flavoured cup, and I drank it to the brim, the bitter and the sweet. I found the sweet bitter and the bitter sweet.' And later in Paris in the last years, he remarked to a friend, 'I wrote when I did not know life, now that I know the meaning of life, I have no more to write.'[4] You have the aesthetic, ascetic, comic, tragic, mystic, Irish, Greek. The last thing I'll quote from is 'The Critic as Artist'. At the end of that essay he says, 'For a dreamer is one who can only find his way by moonlight, and his punishment is that he sees the dawn before the rest of the world.'[5]

3 O. Wilde, 'The Happy Prince' in *Complete Works*, op. cit., pp 271–77 at p. 275. 4 R. Hart-Davis (ed.), *Letters of Oscar Wilde* (London, 1962), p. 828. 5 O. Wilde, 'The Critic as Artist' in *Complete Works*, op. cit., pp 1108-55, at p. 1155.

THOMAS KILROY: One of the fascinating things about Wilde is that he is one of the writers out of the past of whom people are always asking 'What if?' Interest in Ireland is no exception. Every decade when people rediscover Wilde, they always ask, what if he had written more? What if he were writing today? What if he were faced with the gay movement of the twentieth century? This is partly to do with the Keatsian syndrome of someone who stopped writing too young. But how can you explain the extraordinary hold of Wilde over twentieth-century theatre? Has it to do with the quality of comedy, the sheer professionalism of the plays or has it to do with the sensibility of the man? It's a very difficult thing to pin down. I've come up with something, which might be an eccentric description of it. And to do it, I will borrow a line from Lady Windermere when she says, 'Words are merciless.' You remember, there she is talking about the way in which action becomes recorded in words. She says that actions are the first tragedy and words an even greater tragedy. The recording of something is a transformation.

She might be talking about writing, because the imaginative action takes place before the recording of it on the page. Now, in the heat of creativity you might think that this is instantaneous, but, in fact, there is a chasm between moving from one dimension to another. And I think that Wilde as a writer was supremely conscious of the way in which high artifice did something to real life, both in his own life and on the stage. And I think it is a symptom of the type of theatre that he is creating. That particular disjunction between the action and word haunts the twentieth century and its literature. It's the preoccupation of Beckett and, so, in this way, Wilde is a great twentieth-century writer. He is supremely conscious of the mysterious thing that happens when words are used to record human actions. In other words, he is a great stylist.

The other kind of question that Michael Colgan was raising about the Irishness of Wilde and where he fits in is, to me, a fairly simple kind of thing. Wilde is, in fact, part of that great Anglo-Irish theatrical tradition, from Farquhar up to Beckett; and, as part of that tradition, he shares certain qualities of its culture. F.S.L. Lyons used to say the word Anglo-Irish perfectly describes the condition of that culture – its schizophrenia – caught between Anglo and Irish.

There is something of the outsider in the works of these great play-wrights, many of whom directed their attention towards the English comedy of manners, as there is in Wilde observing this world and society in his plays. And, with that outsider thing, there is that wonderful distancing which I admire greatly, and from which I have learned a great deal myself – the way in which, whether you're talking about Farquhar or Yeats or Synge or even Beckett, there is a capacity to have the audience look at something from a distance. What is created is a great space for thought and for reception in the audience itself.

Any playwright who has a strong sense of audience (and Wilde had an inordinate sense of audience) has a tendency to stay within the formula of the day, and Wilde stays within that formula. And, by the time he reached that formula, it was a very tired formula indeed. But, in discovering that type of comedy, he was fortunate to find a couple of things that were very pressing for him personally. One was the whole notion of the secret transgression. There were other things, which he could personalize just as well; and like the great artist that he was, he exhausted that form. *The Importance of Being Earnest* is an exhaustion of that type of comedy because of the perfection of its shape.

PARTICK MASON: One Anglo-Irish writer whom Tom Kilroy forgot to mention was Richard Brinsley Sheridan, and for me there is always this strong parallel between Sheridan's life and work and the life and work of Oscar Wilde. In fact, I believe that when Wilde was first contemplating *The Importance of Being Earnest*, he had a scheme to set it in the eighteenth century. And, if you are ever running a small repertory company, you will find that *The Rivals* by R.B. Sheridan and *The Importance of Being Earnest* by Wilde cross-cast very, very well. I loved Tom's point about the exhaustion of form because Sheridan is the high point of the English comedy of manners, a form kick-started by Farquhar and brought to a kind of perfection at the end of the eighteenth century, but which then outstayed its welcome through the nineteenth century until it reached Oscar Wilde. Wilde took this exhausted, dying form by the scruff of its neck and invested it with not only his own concerns, but with his own personality. That for me is one of the keys to the continual attraction of the plays of Oscar Wilde.

You do experience the man in the work, through the work. To be in the presence of one of the plays is to be, in one sense, in the presence of Oscar Wilde. Everyone sounds like Oscar Wilde. Everyone has that easy wit, that enviable poetry, that extreme perfection of manner.

And yet each one carries both a stereotypical role and a secret meaning. His plays are full of hints, full of these little spaces where things are hidden, where he is flirting with us, where he is seducing us. He is, of course, one of the great performers, and this is why his work in the theatre is still so loved and so vital. He understands, with his masks, that the business of performance is to conceal as much as to reveal, and to titillate an audience with expectation. The buzz in any audience sitting in a theatre waiting to see an Oscar Wilde play is distinctly different from the buzz you will find in any other performance. The very name, as Ellmann points out, is an invitation to fun, to salaciousness, to all kinds of hanky panky. He is a terrific flatterer. I suppose in one sense it's high-class soap. It's more upstairs than downstairs, but he knows that we all wish to be more upstairs than downstairs. Like the best seducer he plays on all those things and brings us into this world. And yet, at the same time, of course, with his love for the paradoxical and his deep knowledge of the paradox as truth, he creates this wonderful dance of veils: he is constantly threatening to tell us who he really is, but he never does.

One of the fascinations intrinsically bound up with the plays 100 years on is more than the contemporary fascination he held as the great wit, the great talker, the great celebrity (he was one of the first media celebrities). For us now, we know the full extent of the man's extraordinary double life, the catastrophic mixture of comedy and tragedy. We know all the contradictions. We know the sexual paradox at the centre of his being. And this gives us an even greater fascination with the man and his work. There have been overtly gay productions of nearly all his plays: cross-dressing, servants as rough trade, Algy and Jack as lovers. The effect of what we know of the life, and the way that life has appealed to us as an utterly modern life, a life of the twentieth and even twenty-first century, the way that that life connects to the plays, has made the plays wonderful brilliant masks that are open to endless interpretations.

One of the other reasons why these plays are so popular is that they are deeply rooted in theatrical cliché (but you could also call them absolute, solid, eternal verities of theatrical performance) – mistaken identities, secret transgressions, discoveries, revelations – the machinery of the theatrical performance all perfectly understood and perfectly deployed, even if you can argue that the form ultimately remains on the wrong side of conservatism. He has no radical solutions to contemporary theatrical forms. He is serious in his intent to take on the new drama, to find out what it has to give him, but there is a sensibility there, paradoxically a strength and a weakness, a west-end sensibility. He has this very shrewd commercial sensibility of what makes popular theatre, theatre of the boulevard.

Now, you can get very snobbish about that and say Beckett is a great artist and Wilde a mere boulevardier. I wonder about this, because even if he is using this form, he is using it with the skill and artistry and intelligence and wit that are extremely hard to match. And greatness? I don't know what greatness is. One of the eternal attractions of Wilde for me is a greatness of heart. Whatever the intellectual brilliance and unmatched wit, there is a generosity in his plays that might be a weakness. You feel he can't quite make people nasty enough to make them real. He likes them all too much. That also engenders warmth in the performance of his plays, and as a warmth it is deeply attractive and seductive. He is one of the most popular playwrights, one of the most playful of playwrights, and the extraordinary paradoxical combination of all the elements of his life and his work will endlessly feed this fascination we have with Wilde. He invites the director to make these links, to explore these links.

MICHAEL COLGAN: I want to ask a question: If, as Tom has said, Wilde had exhausted the form, what would have happened had he continued to write? I go back to Beckett. There are similarities between them both. Both of them made a deliberate decision to write in French because they found that there was a certain burden to writing in English. Both of them were scholars of Trinity. Both of them were exiles. Both of them were adopted by the country of exile and, in some way, lost their Irishness. Both of them were great dramatists. And yet

Beckett wrote work that was more philosophical. And we understand, of course, from what Marina Carr has pointed out from Wilde's academic career that this was something not beyond him. Yet that was not a route he took. I'm wondering if he had had the long writing life that Beckett had, would he have written different plays or would he have continued in that vein? Or, in having exhausted the form, would he have found no other form?

THOMAS KILROY: The thing I was thinking about in relation to *The Importance of Being Earnest* and *Waiting for Godot* is that they have a shared, almost familial, connection. You are aware of several things: you are aware that you are in the presence of a kind of iron ringmaster. And, having said that, and having noted the almost mathematical beauty of each work, you are also dealing with work that has a great deal of human feeling. That is a paradox in itself. You have this kind of severe, almost clinical, quality in the construction and writing and, particularly, in the movements. The manuscripts of Beckett in the Trinity College library show his fascination with, literally, geometric diagrams to map out, on the page, stage movements. You have the same type of qualities in *The Importance of Being Earnest* where things move with a kind of finesse. But inside of that, you have great humour, a great laugh at it all.

PATRICK MASON: In *The Importance of Being Earnest* one of the great unsung heroes is George Alexander, the actor-manager, because it was George Alexander who not only banished Oscar from rehearsals but also edited the play from four acts down to three. And you are absolutely right about the perfection of form, but it was Alexander who sold the form. That's interesting because Wilde was always uneasy about form in the theatre. I think he was troubled by form and convention. He knew that the comedy of manners was exhausted, but I think he felt that that was his gift, his territory. He was intelligent enough to know that there was a whole world of possibilities, but developing that Ibsenite drama didn't suit him.

MICHAEL COLGAN: It's very interesting about form because I remember working with a playwright who had a character of a barking dog in the play. I thought it was very gratuitous and I said to him, 'If you're going to keep this dog coming in you might have introduced him before'. And he said, 'No, no, it's OK to bring him in.' And I remember thinking that it was Oscar Wilde who actually said that plot is something that anyone can do, that it was meaningless. And yet, of all the plays I have produced at the Gate, there has never been anybody who has mastered plot so skilfully. Take *Lady Windermere's Fan*: the extraordinary thing is that there is nobody, not even Shakespeare, who can get a prop and use it for his own selfish needs greater than Oscar.

PATRICK MASON: Oh, I think you are overstating it!

MICHAEL COLGAN: No, I'm not. I'll actually challenge you in this. In *Lady Windermere's Fan*, the play begins with her husband giving her the fan to suggest that it is her birthday, to give a sense of hurrah, celebration, and then there is the sense that he has invited Mrs Erlynne. And what happens when she allows this woman into her house? She drops the fan.

PATRICK MASON: This was a commonplace of Victorian melodrama.

MICHAEL COLGAN: But Oscar used it without any sense of calling the play *Lady Windermere's Fan*. In fact, he was going to call it *The Good Woman*. It was just natural to him and unconscious to him.

PATRICK MASON: But he doesn't resolve it in the way Beckett would. This is the thing: you can't really compare them, because there is one absolutely crucial and extraordinary event that separates both writers, and that happens to be the Second World War. Whatever Beckett's struggles with the novel, he doesn't crack the contemporary theatre form until those terrible years in occupied France and his first-hand and very scary and very bruising experience of the twentieth century with its Gestapo and death camps.

THOMAS KILROY: But Oscar's war was imprisonment. The release failed to release him. He was broken physically and mentally; and he was also broken as a writer.

MICHAEL COLGAN: If the war is the same as imprisonment, can I be controversial and say that *De Profundis* is a bad piece of work.

PATRICK MASON: I don't think it's a bad piece of work; I think it's quite a unique piece of work.

MICHAEL COLGAN: It's an overwritten piece of work.

PATRICK MASON: Quite clearly, because it was Oscar's decision not to edit it. It goes back to my point about George Alexander. Read the four-act version of *The Importance of Being Earnest* and read the three-act version, and just see what George Alexander, one of the great actor-managers of Victorian theatre, just see what he did. He made only one slip-up, and that was a real actor-manager slip-up (because he's tired at the end). There is a crucial little dialogue between Chasuble and Miss Prism and, of course, Alexander takes it out because who was interested in Chasuble and Prism at that stage? Otherwise what he does as an editor is astonishing.

MICHAEL COLGAN: Mindful of the time, I'm going to ask if there are any questions?

QUESTION 1: We have heard a lot about the reclamation of the Irishness of Wilde, but I'm just wondering, to go beyond the box office side of Wilde, why is he so incredibly popular abroad? In many countries, he is the most played of all the dramatists in the English repertory. I think one has to look at what is transcendent in Wilde (rather than just popular) to explain that. Or does one?

MARINA CARR: Wilde said that the impossible in art is anything that happens in real life, and I think he has stuck by that statement in his writing. I think that is probably the main reason why he continues to be seen and read and reinterpreted – he doesn't stick to facts. He says somewhere else that facts should be relegated to the fool's place and not be allowed to take over too much. And I think that, from the point of view of a writer approaching Wilde, there are so many lessons to be learned from him. You have options as a writer, always you have options. You can choose to go with the age and you can choose to go against it. Most of us vacillate somewhere in between. In going against the age, Wilde took what he needed and he moulded it.

PATRICK MASON: I think it's also energy, that quintessential theatrical energy combined with this extraordinary story-telling capacity, and, of course, this amazing breadth of culture. It makes for a very rich kind of performance.

QUESTION 2: I would like to ask the panel why they don't consider that Wilde's work is, in fact, continued and developed through Somerset Maugham and Noel Coward? It seems to me that Wilde flourishes in the twentieth century alongside those writers. He is performed by the same actors, directed by the same directors, and produced by the same producers. There's nothing weird about his survival. That's centrally what west-end theatre was about and Wilde is there all the way through, just like Maugham and Coward and many other people.

PATRICK MASON: Maugham hasn't fared so well – so it's about time for a revival – but Coward is sort of up-and-down; and Coward rather fed off Oscar Wilde. I mean he both parodied Wilde and, I think, did quite a lot of damage to the way in which Wilde is produced and acted because he pioneered or, rather, he perfected that extremely mannered English west-end style. I think it eclipsed the intelligence of Wilde's writing. What is so striking if you compare a play by Oscar Wilde and a play by Noel Coward is how much more intelligent Wilde's play is. Again, I was talking about breadth of culture – there's an intellectual breadth, there's an intellectual brilliance and depth about Wilde which Coward, even at his most charming, doesn't have. Unfortunately, Coward has stood for a long time between Wilde and audiences; that's why I think Wilde is more than just mainstream west-end.

MICHAEL COLGAN: Interestingly, Patrick, the work of Coward would be done more often in London than Oscar Wilde, and the work of Wilde would be done more often in Dublin and in Ireland than Noel Coward.

PATRICK MASON: I think you're right. Dublin and the Gate, I mean, Hilton [Edwards] and Micheál [MacLiammóir], had a relationship with Wilde. Coward, in fact, was very scathing about that when he was here in the 1950s; he was very scathing about these two old queens still pretending they were Oscar Wilde. He saw that as being almost a definition of Dublin as sort of a provincial backwater, that there was still this cult of Oscar Wilde. London had moved on to the cult of Noel Coward of course. But it's very difficult because Wilde is, deliberately, right for the west-end boulevard theatre. But he did subvert it as well. Coward, I don't think, did. Wilde subverted everything. And I think what Coward did was to actually lead to a slightly two-dimensional view of Oscar Wilde.

MICHAEL COLGAN: I'll take one more question.

MERLIN HOLLAND: I'm afraid this is more a statement disguised as a question. If you look at the four social comedies, all of which were written from '92 to '94 at a time when Oscar was desperately in need of money, the ones which worked, the ones where his heart really lay, are the ones which he was going to go on to write at the end of his life. I've always said that his real love lay in what, perhaps, could be considered as the beginning of an experimental theatre. Am I right in thinking this?

THOMAS KILROY: There is one quality in Wilde that is 'very modern', and that is his sense of ritual in theatre. And it's not just simply in *Salomé*. It's actually in the comedies. There are passages in the comedies in which, I think, he plays with ritual, this very self-conscious repetition. In this way, he's doing something with the whole social theme. That was a possibility for future development. Whether his plays would end up with the kind of so called 'poetic expressionism' of the turn of the century, I don't know, but it is something which is very much part of the theatre that followed.

PATRICK MASON: I think, also, that one of the most damaging things about late nineteenth- and early twentieth-century theatre was the pursuit of the poetic drama. The idea of so many writers of that period, that you must revive the poetic drama and these grand poetic themes, is an awful lot of tosh, because the world went the other way, life went the other way. What we have discovered since, of course, is that there is another kind of poetry that is not the great biblical theme or the great purple passage. It's a more austere and dark poetry than any one of them could ever have imagined.

MICHAEL COLGAN: I'd like to leave it at that – with the last question asked by Merlin – so unless there's something really pressing, I just want to thank Patrick, Tom, Marina, and all of you for being here. Thank you very much.

Oscar Wilde's
speech from the dock

LUCY MCDIARMID

The speech from the dock delivered by the young Brendan Behan in *Borstal Boy* ranks high among examples of the form. From the moment of his arrest for carrying the makings of a bomb in his suitcase, Behan shapes his defiance rhetorically. At the CID headquarters, he finishes off his statement with the words of the Manchester Martyrs from the dock: 'God save Ireland.' Later, preparing for his appearance in court, he begins composing a grandiloquent speech: 'My lord and gentlemen, it is my privilege and honour today, to stand, as so many of my countrymen have done, in an English court ...'[1] When he is called before the judge at the Liverpool Assizes, he is interrupted after 'privilege and honour':

> So as this judge was in a vicious and not very judicial temper, I decided to put him in a worse one.
> ' ... and this to a proud and intelligent people, who had a language, a literature, when the barbarian woad-painted Briton was first learning to walk upright.
> 'By plantation, famine, and massacre you have striven to drive the people of Ireland from off the soil of Ireland, but in seven centuries you have not succeeded.
> 'Many times have you announced that you had stamped out the rebels, that "you had terrorism by the throat", that you had settled the "Irish Question".
> 'But there is but the one settlement to the Irish Question, and until the thirty-two-county Republic of Ireland is once more functioning, Ireland unfree shall never be at peace.
> 'God save Ireland. No surrender.'

1 B. Behan, *Borstal Boy* (London, 1990), pp 4, 124. 2 Ibid., pp 136–7.

> The two screws looked at me, and the judge had given up his
> pretence of boredom, and settled himself to sentence me ...
>> He could only sentence me to three years' Borstal Detention.
>> I shouted 'Up the Republic!' across the court and right into
> his face, and went down the stairs in good humour ...[2]

Behan's is the quintessential, paradigmatic speech from the dock for
this reason, that it is so blatantly intertextual. Lloyd George, Patrick
Pearse, and the Manchester Martyrs echo in the lines that bore the
judge. Even the thought of reading speeches from the dock shifts
Behan's discourse into intertextual mode: he instantly begins sounding
like a quotation. 'I often read speeches from the dock', he notes soon
after his arrest, 'and thought the better of the brave and defiant men
that made them so far from friends or dear ones.'[3]

Of course the whole point of an Irish patriot's speech from the dock is
its intertextuality. The textual tradition links the patriots across the years,
and the continuing sequence of linked speeches serves as an accumulating
collective memory of political resistance and confirms the tradition. The
1867 publication of the Sullivan brothers' book, *Speeches from the Dock*,
preserved and enshrined the tradition, thereby assuring its continuity.[4]
The rituals of that tradition require Behan to claim his patriotic identity
in an in-your-face speech through which the voices of the dead are also
heard. Roger Casement, in the first sentence of his speech from the dock,
explains that he wants to read his remarks because he wishes to reach a
larger audience than the one he can see before him in the court.[5] It was
the written, not the oral, tradition in which he sought immortality. At a
later point in *Borstal Boy*, Behan meets another IRA member who says,
'That was a great speech you made altogether. I saw it in the papers.'[6] The
dock-speakers are always conscious of the audience, and the audience
conscious of the tradition. Needless to say, this is not a tradition universally admired: the Irish-American lawyer John Quinn said scornfully of

---

3 Ibid., p. 4.   4 T.D. Sullivan, A.M. Sullivan, and D.B. Sullivan, *Speeches from the Dock, or
Protests of Irish Patriotism* (Dublin, 1867).   5 See the complete version printed in B. Inglis,
Roger Casement (Belfast, 1993), pp 421–31, beginning, 'My Lord Chief Justice, as I wish to
reach a much wider audience than I see before me here, I intend to read all that I propose
to say.'   6 B. Behan, *Borstal Boy*, op. cit., p. 185.

the 1916 rebels that he was sure each of them went out with a speech from the dock up his sleeve.[7]

PATRIOTS & CELEBRITIES

Current orthodoxy holds that Oscar Wilde's deportment during and after his trial reflects this patriotic paradigm. Terry Eagleton's 1989 play, *Saint Oscar*, gives Wilde a more self-consciously traditional speech from the dock, one closer in its staginess, if not in its diction, to those in the Sullivan collection. Eagleton's Wilde complains that an Irishman can't 'receive a fair hearing in an English court' and asks for a jury of 'poets, perverts, vagrants and geniuses'.[8] Seamus Heaney's essay on 'The Ballad of Reading Gaol' in *The Redress of Poetry* speaks approvingly of Eagleton's interpretation and reads Speranza's political interests into Wilde's final poem. Heaney observes, 'Wilde had been magnificent in the dock and had conducted himself with as much dramatic style as any Irish patriot ever did.'[9] Recently on BBC 2 Tom Paulin said of Wilde,

> His mother was a leading Irish nationalist poet so really he was programmed to take the trajectory that is part of the culture, and that is to end up in the dock, be sentenced, taken to jail, make a brilliant series of speeches from the dock, and to be remembered as a martyr. Now he is a great gay martyr but he is following also the trajectory of so many Irish republicans.[10]

The Irish rebel paradigm is the wrong paradigm for Wilde, however, and it's that orthodoxy I'd like to argue against. It's only Wilde *in the dock* that I intend to dehibernicize, not Wilde's writings and certainly not the Irish nationalist convictions he held all his life. Wilde himself noted many 'Celtic' elements in his writing and in his personality, and he was a passionate Home Ruler who believed that 'Ireland should rule England'.[11] Jerusha McCormack's *Wilde the Irishman* contains the eloquent testimo-

---

7 B.L. Reid, *The Man from New York: John Quinn and His Friends* (New York, 1968), p. 232. 8 T. Eagleton, *Saint Oscar* (Derry, 1989), p. 46. 9 S. Heaney, 'Speranza in Reading Gaol', *The Redress of Poetry* (New York, 1995), p. 95. 10 Tom Paulin's comments were made on *Artzone*, BBC 2, 5 November 2000. 11 T. Wratislaw, *Oscar Wilde: A Memoir* (London, 1979), p. 13.

ny of many critics to Wilde's Irishness.[12] I wouldn't deny them. Nor am I attempting to disassociate Wilde from Irish rebels: it's a passion for accuracy that drives me to make this case. Anyone who goes back and forth between the Montgomery Hyde book of the Wilde trials and the Sullivans' *Speeches from the Dock* cannot fail to notice how completely unlike the Irish patriots Wilde sounds.[13] It's clear that Wilde in the dock is not speaking from consciousness of any explicit, labellable, consistent ideology. It's also clear that he did not wish to be a martyr or to die for any cause. And the 'cause' that Paulin associates Wilde with and makes analogous to Irish republicanism, gay sexuality, is one Wilde repeatedly and consistently denied association with *while he was in the dock*.

The right paradigm for Wilde is another one, one that's different in a subtle but important way. It's a paradigm based on the behaviour and attitudes of a group I call, for want of a better term, *oppositional celebrities*. Its chief exemplars are Byron, Wilfrid Blunt, and T.E. Lawrence; its original is Milton's Satan. One of its minor exemplars is R.B. Cunninghame Graham. There are loose links, social and literary, among the figures whose names I've mentioned: Byron was a great admirer of Milton's Satan and (like Blake) considered him the 'hero' of *Paradise Lost*. Blunt was an admirer of Byron and married his granddaughter, Lady Anne Noel. Wilde, writing to the French translator of 'Reading Gaol,' explained the word 'outcast' by saying, 'Lord Byron *était un* "outcast".'[14] Wilde reviewed Blunt's prison poems (written in Galway Gaol) and famously said that 'Prison has had an admirable effect on Mr Wilfrid Blunt as a poet'.[15] The series of prison poems written by Blunt was titled *In vinculis*, and the original title of *De Profundis*, the title Wilde gave it, was *Epistola: in carcere et in vinculis*. Wilde was also a member of Blunt's 'Crabbet Club'.[16] T.E. Lawrence, also a friend of Blunt's, called him a 'Prophet'.[17] Cunninghame Graham was a friend of both Lawrence and Blunt, and he was a great

12 J. McCormack (ed.), *Wilde the Irishman* (New Haven and London, 1998). See also R. Haslam, 'Oscar Wilde and the Imagination of the Celt', *Irish Studies Review*, 11 (Summer 1995), 2–5. 13 H.M. Hyde, *The Trials of Oscar Wilde* (New York, 1962). 14 O. Wilde, letter to Henry D. Davray (April 1898), *The Complete Letters of Oscar Wilde* eds. Merlin Holland & Rupert Hart-Davis (New York, 2000), p. 1053. 15 O. Wilde, 'Poetry and Prison', *The Artist as Critic*, ed. Richard Ellman (Chicago, 1982), p. 116. 16 E. Longford, *A Pilgrimage of Passion: The Life of Wilfrid Scawen Blunt* (London, 1979), pp 289–91. 17 Ibid., p. 418.

admirer of 'Ballad of Reading Gaol'; he, too, had written about his time in prison.[18]

For the oppositional celebrities, the paradigm is not to have a paradigm. The model they follow directs them to appear free, unpredictable, improvisational, to shock and to surprise an enthralled public; to claim this lineage and yet to insist on uniqueness and revel in eccentricity. In *De Profundis* Wilde compares himself to Byron because both are what he calls 'symbolic figures' for their ages, but (notes Wilde) Byron's 'relations were to the passion of his age ... Mine were to something more noble, more permanent, of more vital issue, of larger scope.'[19] Nor can oppositional celebrities be stabilized in one mode: all of them vacillate between 'sin' and what 'Ballad of Reading Gaol' calls 'the wild regrets'; and between being 'outcast' from Society and being a guest in the drawing rooms of the rich and powerful. They form a sharp contrast to the patriots in many respects. They don't have a single-minded dedication to one 'cause'; it's the idea of ideology that attracts them, but not just one. Instead of passionate and unambiguous commitment, they manifest a general and glamorous oppositionality that is ludic and provocative. It's not *Tiocfaidh ár Lá* with them but *épater le bourgeois*.

The domestic lives of the Irish patriots and the oppositional celebrities also differ considerably. Most of the Young Irelanders and Fenians had conventional sexual lives and domestic arrangements. For the celebrities, conventional domesticity was fine in its place (at home), and they liked to have it there waiting for them, but outside it they enjoyed any of a number of transgressive sexualities, in Byron's case all of them. They were louche seducers, charmers, *roués*, continental rather than English in their pleasures, surrounded by an aura of eroticism (and of French phrases). Their whole style and *mentalité* were different from those of the Irish rebels who followed the 'trajectory' Paulin alluded to on television. They weren't 'respectable'; they were shocking. They had a histrionic sense of their own importance, especially when they were engaged in noble political work. When Byron set off for Greece, he had 'splendid uniforms and dramatic plumed helmets' made for himself and an Italian companion,

18 Ibid., pp 157, 418. Wilde, Letter to Robert Ross [? 20 February 1898], *Complete Letters*, op. cit., pp 1021–2 and n1024.   19 O. Wilde, Letter to Lord Alfred Douglas (aka *De Profundis*) [January–March 1897], *Complete Letters*, op. cit., p. 729.

his own 'flaunting the family motto "Crede Byron"'.[20] In fact clothing, fashion, and hairstyle were inseparable from their political stances. The visible was of paramount importance to all of them; they all liked to be painted and photographed and seen. A large part of their anti-imperializing was staged to shock the folks back home: whatever they were doing, they were always looking back over their shoulder at the London papers to see the headlines and pictures of their own exploits.

Blunt's arrest in Galway in 1887 is a case in point: he was on a platform speaking at a banned anti-eviction meeting, and the local magistrate and police pulled him down. He got back up and again started speaking. They pulled him down again. Then he got up and taunted them: 'Are you all such damned cowards that not one of you dares arrest me?' They had no choice; and they accommodated Blunt, thereby making the day one that 'deserves to be remembered in Irish history,' Blunt wrote, because it was the 'first recorded instance' of an Englishman's being imprisoned for Ireland.[21] The credit for this accomplishment surely belongs less to the sovereignty goddess than to Blunt's understanding of media interest in the theatrics of protest. A sketch of the platform episode soon appeared on the front of the *London Illustrated News*, but the event's significance in Irish history has been superseded by later, more extreme sacrifices.[22]

Finally, in the rebel paradigm there is a commitment to the cause of Ireland no matter what sacrifice or martyrdom is entailed. The oppositional celebrities, however, enjoy living dangerously; they're reckless. They live on the edge; but they're not in a hurry to die. Making their final and fatal choices, both Byron and Wilde were ambivalent: Byron would have turned back from Greece if he hadn't been afraid of looking ridiculous in the eyes of all the people he'd told he was going; and Wilde had a 'half-packed suitcase' at the Cadogan.[23] Blunt managed to survive his adventures, as did Lawrence. This paradigm doesn't offer any particular guidelines about what to do in extreme circumstances, but it privileges staying-alive-to-be-talked-about-and-photographed over martyrdom. For Wilde on trial, there was no trajectory to follow, no single claim on his ideolog-

---

20 P. Grosskurth, *Byron: the Flawed Angel* (Boston & New York, 1997), p. 430. 21 *London Illustrated News*, Saturday 5 November 1887, p. 531. 22 E. Longford, *A Pilgrimage of Passion*, op. cit., pp 251–2. 23 R. Ellmann, *Oscar Wilde* (London, 1988), p. 429.

ical allegiance, no tradition to determine his answers in the dock. He had to improvize, and it's as an improvisationalist that he must be understood during his trial.

WILDES IN THE DOCK

The Wilde family tradition valorized a proud and defiant stance in the dock, but there were no family martyrs. As a female cultural nationalist among militant male nationalists, Oscar Wilde's mother, Speranza, was able to express her faithful devotion to a cause without serious concern that she would have to die for it. She thought of herself as a celebrity and to that end organized her own complete makeover. Her name, her fashions, and her politics were carefully constructed to create a flamboyant and eccentric identity. Her flamboyance and eccentricity and talents were put at the service of the nation, subordinated to a single unambiguous ideology. When Paulin said that Wilde's 'mother was a leading Irish nationalist poet so really he was programmed to take the trajectory', he may have been thinking of the dedication of the 1864 edition of her *Poems*, which reads, 'Dedicated to My Sons Willie and Oscar Wilde,' with the following lines: 'I made them indeed, / Speak plain the word COUNTRY. I taught them, no doubt,/ That a Country's a thing men should die for at need!'[24] Or he may have been thinking of what Lady Wilde famously said to her younger son before his trials: 'If you stay, even if you go to prison, you will always be my son. It will make no difference to my affection. But if you go, I will never speak to you again.'[25] Speranza spoke the language of patriotism, but in her own life, style and celebrity had always sufficed.

At Charles Gavan Duffy's treason trial in 1848 Speranza had indeed spoken plain, although, like the young Brendan Behan, she wasn't given the opportunity to make a big speech. Her involvement in the trial was indirect: one of the offences listed in the indictment against Gavan Duffy was publication in *The Nation* of two articles actually written by Speranza, 'The Hour of Destiny' and 'Jacta Alea Est'. In the former she wrote,

24 Speranza (Lady Wilde), *Poems* (Dublin & London, 1864), dedication page (unnumbered). 25 W.B. Yeats, *Autobiographies* (New York, 1965), p. 192.

> Ireland! Ireland! It is no petty insurrection – no local quarrel – no
> party triumph that summons you to the field. The destinies of the
> world – the advancement of the human race – depends now on
> your courage and success ... It is a death struggle between the
> oppressor and the slave – between the murderer and his victim.[26]

And in the latter:

> 'Oh! for a hundred thousand muskets glittering brightly in the
> light of Heaven ... '[27]

Speranza was in the gallery throughout the trial, which ended after
numerous mistrials in a hung jury. On the 21st of February, when the
Solicitor-General mentioned 'Jacta Alea Est,' Speranza attempted to make
her complicity known. According to a contemporary account,

> A lady who occupied during the trial a seat in the gallery here rose
> and said to Mr Hatchell, 'I beg your pardon, but I wish to say –'
> (The remainder of the sentence was lost amid the cries of silence,
> and the directions of police-officers etc. to 'stop that interruption.')
> The Solicitor-General observed that it had been intimated to him
> that his article was written by a lady. He went on to say that it was
> incumbent on the prisoner to prove that he had no knowledge of
> it, had nothing to do with it.[28]

At this point again the 'lady' tried to speak: she began 'He never –' but
was interrupted by a policeman standing near her. Although Gavan Duffy
finally said that he wanted to take the 'entire responsibility' for the article,
Speranza had at least the pleasure of seeing her intervention in the trial
become legendary. By the time *Irish Society* was telling the story, her inter-
ruption had been lengthened to the eloquent line, 'I am the culprit, if culprit there be.'[29] To a friend, Speranza wrote, 'if an illustrated history of
Ireland is published no doubt I shall be immortalized in the act of

26 'The Hour of Destiny', *The Nation* (22 July 1848), 473.   27 'Jacta Alea Est', *The Nation*
(29 July 1848), 488.   28 T. de Vere White, *The Parents of Oscar Wilde, Sir William and Lady
Wilde* (London, 1967), pp 108–9.   29 'Our Irish Portrait Gallery: Lady Wilde', *Irish Society*
(31 December 1892), 1269–70.

addressing the court.'[30] Like Byron and Blunt, Speranza liked to think of herself being gazed at by posterity.

Oscar Wilde's own trials for 'acts of gross indecency' do not actually resemble the Gavan Duffy treason trial, with its Young Ireland colleagueality, open patriotism, and happy ending (no jury would convict him). Wilde's trials do, however, resemble the Mary Travers libel trial of 1864. On that occasion, the twenty-eight-year old Miss Travers sued Lady Wilde for libel because of a letter written to Miss Travers' father, which seemed to imply that Miss Travers hung out with newspaper boys. During the course of the trial, Miss Travers accused Sir William of raping her while she visited him in his office as his patient. Some kind of hanky-panky had indeed taken place, and foolish, infatuated, anxious letters from Sir William to Miss Travers were read aloud. Although the court held that she had been libelled, she was awarded only a farthing in damages.[31] In the anger and vengeance that inspired it, in its outing of private, extra-marital sexual passions, in the attempt to expose to ridicule and to ruin a famous citizen, in its sleazy atmosphere and prolonged unpleasantness, this is the trial that more accurately anticipates what Wilde endured in the spring of 1895.

If in fact there had been collective memory of earlier eighteenth- and nineteenth-century male homosexual scandals; if Wilde had alluded in his testimony to the 1870 Boulton-Park case, in which two young men were 'arrested for dressing as women' and later tried for 'conspiring to commit sodomy'; and if Wilde had given a speech openly and unapologetically acknowledging his homosexual activities, and invoking as a genealogy all the previous defendants in such trials – then he would be the gay martyr Eagleton and Paulin turn him into.[32] But there was no such collective memory: the law under which he was prosecuted, the notorious Labouchère amendment to the Criminal Law Amendment Act, didn't exist till 1885. The genealogy, as Alan Sinfield has shown in *The Wilde Century*, begins with Wilde.[33] Wilde did not have it to draw on: there was

30 J. Melville, *Mother of Oscar: The Life of Jane Francesca Wilde* (London, 1994), p. 39.   31 T. de Vere White, *Parents of Oscar Wilde*, op. cit., p. 200.   32 For an analysis of the Boulton-Park case, I am grateful to William A. Cohen for a copy of his unpublished talk 'Scandal before Wilde: The Boulton/Park Affair'.   33 A. Sinfield, *The Wilde Century: Effeminacy, Oscar Wilde and the Queer Movement* (New York, 1994).

no intertextual tradition available. Nor did the paradigm of oppositional celebrity offer any model for what such a person should do when faced with the terrible prospect of utter ruin and two years' hard labour. There was no model: so Wilde had to improvise.

The closest thing to a formal 'speech from the dock' that Wilde gave is the eloquent apologia that served as his response to prosecutor Charles Gill's question about Lord Alfred Douglas' poem, 'What is the "Love that dare not speak its name"?'

> 'The love that dare not speak its name' in this century is such a great affection of an elder for a younger man as there was between David and Jonathan, such as Plato made the very basis of his philosophy, and such as you find in the sonnets of Michelangelo and Shakespeare. It is that deep, spiritual affection that is as pure as it is perfect. It dictates and pervades great works of art like those of Shakespeare and Michelangelo, and those two letters of mine, such as they are. It is in this century misunderstood, so much misunderstood that it may be described as the 'Love that dare not speak its name', and on account of it I am placed where I am now. It is beautiful, it is fine, it is the noblest form of affection. There is nothing unnatural about it. It is intellectual, and it repeatedly exists between an elder and a younger man, when the elder has intellect, and the younger man has all the joy, hope, and glamour of life before him. That it should be so, the world does not understand. The world mocks at it and sometimes puts one in the pillory for it.[34]

According to Montgomery Hyde's account,

> Wilde's words produced a spontaneous outburst of applause from the public gallery, mingled with some hisses, which moved the judge to say he would have the Court cleared if there were any further manifestation of feeling. There is no doubt, however, that what Wilde said made an unforgettable impression on all those who heard him, not least the jury. The incident also seemed to give Wilde renewed self-confidence in the witness box.[35]

34 H.M. Hyde, *Trials of Oscar Wilde*, op. cit., p. 201.   35 Ibid.

Although this effusion was new and exciting to the people in the court, it was not entirely new to Wilde. Some measure of the applause must have come from admiration for apparently extemporaneous eloquence, but Wilde – lacking the tradition for sexuality that Behan had for republicanism – was quoting what he himself had said in a previous improvisational moment. He had given the speech, or something close to it, in 1891 as part of the curious hazing ritual of Wilfrid Blunt's Crabbet Club, a 'convivial association' of forty-five men who met annually at Blunt's family estate in Crabbet Park. Each new member, before his election, had to have a devil's advocate, and Wilde's was George Curzon. In the presence of all the other members of the club, Curzon (recorded Blunt) played 'with astonishing audacity and skill upon [Wilde's] reputation for sodomy'. As Wilde stood up to reply, Blunt felt sorry for him, but Wilde soon 'pulled himself together ... and gradually warmed into an amusing and excellent speech'. Four years later, during the second trial, 'Oscar's line of defence' (wrote Blunt) 'was precisely the same as that made in his impromptu speech that evening at Crabbet'.[36]

Nor was the speech at Crabbet entirely off-the-cuff: Wilde was quoting his own words, published that very year in *The Picture of Dorian Gray*. When Dorian Gray thinks of Basil Hallward's love for him, a love that 'would have helped him to resist Lord Henry's influence,' he characterizes it in terms of its historical precedents:

> The love that he bore him – for it was really love – had nothing in it that was not noble and intellectual. It was not that mere physical admiration of beauty that is born of the senses, and that dies when the senses tire. It was such love as Michael Angelo had known, and Montaigne, and Winckelmann, and Shakespeare himself. Yes, Basil could have saved him.[37]

In both of its pre-trial contexts, the genealogical trope served to distinguish mere venereal homosexual love – the 'sodomy' Curzon accused Wilde of, the poisonous influences' of Lord Henry – from a love that was 'noble and intellectual.'[38] In the trope, this higher love is legitimized, elevated, even sacralized, by its association with great figures of western culture.

36 E. Longford, *A Pilgrimage of Passion*, op. cit., p. 290. 37 O. Wilde, *The Picture of Dorian Gray* (London, 1985), p. 132. 38 See also A. Sinfield, *Cultural Politics – Queer Reading*

In creating the genealogies in *The Picture of Dorian Gray* and the speech in his trial, Wilde was constructing a tradition out of the male artists and writers analyzed and celebrated by the aesthetes: Pater (Michelangelo, Winckelmann), John Addington Symonds (Plato, Michelangelo) and himself (Shakespeare). Wilde thus introduced into popular, extra-literary discourse, in one grand gesture, the more elite and academic discourses of Pater and Symonds. Pater's *Studies in the History of the Renaissance* had first been published in 1873; Symonds' *A Problem in Greek Ethics* had been privately printed in an edition of ten copies in 1883, and his *A Problem in Modern Ethics* had been privately printed in 1891. There was already an intertextual tradition here: Pater had used Symonds' translations of Michelangelo, and Symonds had reviewed Pater's *Renaissance*.[39] Pater had influenced Symonds, and Symonds Wilde, on the Greeks. Wilde was one of twelve people to whom Symonds sent his translations of Michelangelo's sonnets.[40] Symonds' *Italian By-ways* was one of the books on Wilde's 'wish list' sent to Robbie Ross from Reading in 1897.[41] And of course all three were connected through Oxford, where, as Richard Dellamora and Linda Dowling have argued, a hellenizing discourse was increasingly associated with same-sex love.[42] From these private friendships and discrete scholarly exchanges, as well as from Wilde's own *Portrait of Mr W. H.* (1889), evolved the thinking that had emerged into print in *The Picture of Dorian Gray*, into private-sphere speech at Blunt's Crabbet Club, and that burst finally into the public sphere in the open courtroom in 1895. Collating these traditions, speaking them in public when challenged, Wilde uttered, in Dowling's words, 'a new language of moral legitimacy pointing forward to Anglo-American decriminalization and, ultimately, a fully developed assertion of homosexual rights'.[43]

(Philadelphia, 1994), p. 64: 'Oscar Wilde's celebrated speech about the love that dare not speak its name ... is justifying non-sexual love.'   **39** A. Potts, 'Pungent Prophecies of Art: Symonds, Pater, and Michelangelo', in J. Pemble (ed.), *John Addington Symonds: Culture and the Demon Desire* (London, 2000), pp 102–21 at p. 103.   **40** R. Ellmann, *Oscar Wilde*, op. cit., p. 31.   **41** O. Wilde, Letter to Robert Ross, 6 April [1897], *Complete Letters*, op. cit., p. 792.   **42** R. Dellamora, *Masculine Desire: The Sexual Politics of Victorian Aestheticism* (Chapel Hill, 1990) and 'Dorianism', *Apocalyptic Overtures* (New Brunswick, 1994), pp 43–64; L. Dowling, *Hellenism and Homosexuality in Victorian Oxford* (Ithaca, 1994).   **43** L. Dowling, *Hellenism and Homosexuality*, op. cit., p. 2.

As the originator of a courtroom tradition that enabled him to claim a sacred genealogy for his identity, Wilde could not draw on the kind of broad popular recognition that the typical Irish martyr received from his listening and reading audiences. This was novelty and brilliant improvisation, not a subordination of personal identity to a pre-existing larger cause for which heroes had already died. Robert Emmet, speaking from the dock after his failed rebellion in 1803, had invoked his dead predecessors:

> When my spirit shall be wafted to a more friendly port – when my shade shall have joined the banks of those martyred heroes who have shed their blood on the scaffold and in the field in the defence of their country ... – I wish that my memory and name may animate those who survive me.[44]

Speaking from the dock in 1865, John O'Leary invoked Emmet, as 'Captain Mackey' (aka William Frances Lomasney) in the dock in 1868 invoked the words of the Manchester martyr Michael Larkin.[45] Not only did Wilde invent a tradition; the names he invoked were not martyrs but iconic figures of western culture, men who had died of natural causes, unpunished for any homoerotic passions: David and Jonathan, Plato, Michelangelo, Shakespeare.

As Dowling has observed, Wilde was answering the legal language in which sodomy was imagined 'as belonging to a forbidden range of merely genital practices having no essential connection to personal identity':

> Wilde's triumph in the war of discourses symbolized by his exchanges with the Crown prosecutor was to have equated this thoroughly modern notion of personal identity with the ideal of male love surviving in the writings of ancient Greece.[46]

He was describing 'an idea of male love as a mode of inward erotic orientation and sensibility wholly distinct from mere genital activity'.[47] But the very distinction built into the homosexual genealogy in Wilde's other uses

---

44 T.D. Sullivan, A.M. Sullivan, and D.B. Sullivan, *Speeches from the Dock, or Protests of Irish Patriotism* (Boston, 1878), pp 46–7. 45 Ibid., pp 170, 236. 46 L. Dowling, *Hellenism and Homosexuality*, op. cit., pp 2, 3. 47 Ibid., p. 3.

of it, that between 'sodomy' or 'poisonous influences' and a nobler love, serves in this instance a different purpose. It exonerates Wilde from guilt of the crimes as charged. The speech was delivered during the second of Wilde's three trials; he was defending himself against the charge of 'acts of gross indecency'. In the immediate context, Charles Gill asked Wilde if the 'loves' described in Lord Alfred Douglas' poem were 'natural love and unnatural love'. When Wilde answered 'No,' Gill then asked the question that triggered the speech about 'the "Love that dare not speak its name"'. To say 'There is nothing unnatural about it. It is intellectual', is in the immediate legal context to deny the love's illegality. The speech not only created a genealogy for homoerotic love; it sanitized and desexualized it. The jury must have been persuaded, because it was the only one of three juries judging Wilde in the course of his trials that did not find him guilty.

Given Wilde's privately acknowledged guilt, he differs significantly from the Irish rebels who defiantly and publicly accepted responsibility for their actions. Thomas Francis Meagher, on trial in 1848, proclaimed, 'I am here to speak the truth, whatever it may cost – I am here to regret nothing I have ever done ... I am here to crave with no lying lip the life I consecrate to the liberty of my country.'[48] In its drama, its *éclat,* in its power to inspire a courtroom audience, Wilde's speech resembles those of Irish patriots. As Heaney says, Wilde 'had been magnificent in the dock and had conduct- ed himself with as much dramatic style as any Irish patriot'.[49] But where the Irish patriots accepted the higher criminality of their militant nation- alism, Wilde defines his 'love' in a way that insists on his innocence.

CIVILIZING THE COMMUNITY

For all the considerable evidence Wilde was confronted with in the trials – the dirty sheets, the engraved silver cigarette cases, the watches and chains, the shirts, the champagne and brandy and coffee – for all the material indications of relationships, Wilde had to improvise theories that offered non-erotic explanations. At one point in the first trial, Carson elicited the fact that Wilde had invited Alfred Taylor to dinner on his

48 T.D. Sullivan, et al., *Speeches from the Dock*, op. cit., 1878, p. 141. 49 S. Heaney, *Redress of Poetry*, op. cit., p. 95.

birthday and had told Taylor to invite his friends. The friends were Charlie Parker and his brother William.

> 'Did you know that one, Parker, was a gentleman's valet, and the other a groom?' Carson asked sneeringly. 'I did not know it,' Wilde answered with conviction, 'but if I had I should not have cared. I didn't care tuppence what they were. I liked them. I have a passion to civilize the community.'[50]

In improvizing this answer to explain intimate cross-class friendships, Wilde drew on a contemporary social practice that he didn't name, but that was familiar to his Victorian contemporaries. That practice is the 'rescue,' in which educated, idealistic and socially progressive middle- and upper-middle class people befriended and sought to 'improve' poor people such as the 'street arabs' alluded to in the trial. 'Do I understand' (Carson demanded of Wilde) 'that even a young boy you might pick up in the street would be a pleasing companion?' 'I would talk to a street arab, with pleasure', Wilde responded.[51]

Many of the professional reformers active in rescue efforts were linked with Oxford. As Seth Koven has written,

> T.H. Green, the leading Oxford Idealist philosopher, offered ... the most subtle and influential formulation of the problem of male citizenship, class and culture in the 1870s and 80s. The citizen was the man who stood above the prejudices of class, who performed his sacred duties for the benefit of the entire community and nation. Green asked that in exchange for the full privileges of membership in the political nation, working men should abandon class conflict in favour of harmonious and consensual social politics.[52]

In 1893, Hugh Legge, 'a recent graduate of Trinity College, Oxford, arrived in the heart of the slums of East London ... to live among the poor as a resident in Oxford House', a recently established settlement house.

50 H.M. Hyde, *Trials of Oscar Wilde*, op. cit., p. 127. 51 Ibid., p. 129. 52 S. Koven, 'From Rough Lads to Hooligans: Boy Life, National Culture and Social Reform', in A. Parker (ed.), *Nationalisms and Sexualities* (New York and London, 1992), p. 367.

The 'men's settlement movement' consciously attempted 'to create nation and community through vertical bonds of comradeship across class lines'.[53] Through clubs, settlement houses, classes, and other activities bourgeois men become close friends with poor urban 'lads'.

What would Carson have said to these charitable men, had he had them in the dock? He might have had a lot to say, or at least to suspect. 'Through a wide range of morally uplifting and physically wholesome cultural and sporting activities', Koven notes,

> reformers sought to reconstitute 'manly' communities with one another and with rough lads in the slums of London. However, their relationships with rough lads were neither as unproblematic nor as innocent as this account suggests. Their own writings, published and private, suggest deep if sometimes contradictory connections between their objects of social reform and their objects of sexual desire. Just as the reformers' democratic rhetoric about the creation of a common culture conflicted with their elitist political and economic agendas, so too their desires for rough lads led some to doubt their own 'moral purity'.[54]

Such ambiguity was articulated often and was a familiar public complaint. Girls as well as boys were considered vulnerable to the aggressive intimacies of the charitably-inclined bourgeois. The classic literary text on this subject had not been written in 1895, when Wilde was on trial, but it was written 18 years later by Wilde's friend, Bernard Shaw. Its name was *Pygmalion*, and like the *Symposium*, to which I don't believe it has ever been compared, it shows the fuzzy border between pedagogic and erotic relationships. In *Pygmalion*, as Henry Higgins' flower girl comes to live in his house, erotic issues are constantly being raised in the text of the play, by every one of the characters except Higgins himself – by Eliza Doolittle, by Colonel Pickering, by Alfred Doolittle, Higgins' housekeeper, and his mother – but they are never acted on. Higgins' passion, like Wilde's, was 'a passion to civilize'. Higgins, too, has a great white canon to invoke: the language Eliza is ruining, he tells her, is 'the language of Shakespear [sic] and Milton, and the Bible'.[55]

53 Ibid., p. 365. 54 Ibid., pp 374–5. 55 Act I, *Pygmalion, A Romance in Five Acts* (1912) in *The Complete Plays of Bernard Shaw* (London, 1965), pp 716–57, at p. 72.

Even, then, for those not engaged in 'acts of gross indecency' with rent-boys, the practice of 'rescues' is sexually fraught. With this history in mind, look again at Carson's cross-examination about Wilde's friendship with young Alphonse Conway:

'What was he?'
'He led a happy, idle life.'
'He was a loafer, in fact?'
'He seemed to me to be just enjoying life.'
'How old was he?'
'He was a youth of about eighteen.'

Asked how he had made his acquaintance, Wilde explained that when he and Lord Alfred Douglas were at Worthing they used to go out in a boat. One day young Conway helped the fisherman to get the craft into the water and Wilde suggested that they should ask Conway to come for a sail. Douglas agreed, and after that Conway and Wilde became great friends. Wilde admitted that he had asked him to lunch, and also that Conway had dined with him at his house and lunched with him at the Marine Hotel.

*   *   *   *   *

'He was a simple country lad?'
'He was a nice, pleasant creature. His mother kept a lodging-house, and his desire was to go to sea ... '

*   *   *

Pressed further about the nature of his relations with Conway, Wilde emphatically denied that he had met him by appointment one evening and taken him along the road towards Lancing, 'kissing him and indulging in familiarities on the way'. He also denied that he had ever given him any money, but he admitted that he had given him a cigarette case ('Alphonse from his friend Oscar Wilde'), a signed photograph of himself, and a book called *The Wreck of the Grosvenor*.

With a sudden dramatic gesture, Carson produced these gifts, together with a silver-mounted walking-stick, which Wilde had not mentioned, and held them up for the inspection of the jury. The faces of the twelve good men and true in the jury-box plainly showed signs of surprise.

'Were you fond of this boy?' continued Carson.

'Naturally,' Wilde answered ... 'He had been my companion for six weeks.'

* * *

'Did you take the lad to Brighton?'

'Yes.'

'And provided him with a suit of blue serge?'

'Yes.'

'And a straw hat with a band of red and blue?'

'That, I think was his unfortunate selection.'

'But you paid for it?'

'Yes.'

'You dressed this newsboy up to take him to Brighton?'

'No. I did not want him to be ashamed of his shabby clothes.'

'In order that he might look more like an equal?'

'Oh, no! He could not look like that. No, I promised him that before I left Worthing I would take him somewhere ... as a reward for his being a pleasant companion to myself and my children ... We dined at a restaurant and stayed the night at the Albion Hotel, where I took a sitting-room and two bedrooms.'

'Did the bedrooms communicate by a green baize door?'

'I am not sure.'[56]

In *Pygmalion*, similar ambiguities do *not* hide an erotic relationship: Eliza, also, is re-dressed more fashionably, wined and dined and enabled to 'pass' as upper middle-class. (Both Alphonse and Eliza are said by their peda-gogues to have bad taste in hats.) Of course Alphonse Conway is not a street arab, or a Londoner; his father had been an 'electrical engineer,' according to Wilde's testimony. But the activity of bourgeoisifying, with all its attendant dangers, is the same. In this cross-examination as in so many of the others, Wilde improvised, here drawing on contemporary charitable practices to recontextualize the evidence.

56 H.M. Hyde, *Trials of Oscar Wilde*, op. cit., pp 121–3.

'THE BALLAD OF READING GAOL'

The improvisations didn't persuade the jury in the third trial, and Wilde was sentenced to two years' hard labour. As a prisoner, Wilde didn't have the power to make his transgressions seem witty, provocative, and ludic. Instead of the 'notoriety' he had once joked about wanting, he had infamy. For someone whose politics had always been focussed on the visible drama of his own life, visibility became a form of torture, as this passage from *De Profundis* shows:

> On 13th November 1895 I was brought down here [Reading Gaol] from London. From two o'clock till half-past two on that day I had to stand on the centre platform of Clapham Junction in convict dress, and handcuffed, for the world to look at. I had been taken out of the hospital ward without a moment's notice being given to me. Of all possible objects I was the most grotesque. When people saw me they laughed. Each train as it came up swelled the audience. Nothing could exceed their amusement. That was, of course, before they knew who I was. As soon as they had been informed they laughed still more. For half an hour I stood there in the grey November rain surrounded by a jeering mob. For a year after that was done to me I wept everyday at the same hour.[57]

In the dock, Wilde had said of the 'Love that dare not speak its name' that 'the world mocks at it and sometimes puts one in the pillory for it'. Yet in this painful passage Wilde does not formulate his misery as ideologically meaningful.

Nor had Wilde made ideological meaning out of his experiences at the time (two years later) when he wrote 'The Ballad of Reading Gaol'. Heaney says that in that poem Wilde 'converted himself into the kind of propagandist poet his mother had been fifty years before', but only ten stanzas out of 109, nine per cent of the poem, attack the inhumanities of the prison system.[58] The poem doesn't celebrate a great public cause: the

---

57 O. Wilde, *Complete Letters*, op. cit., pp 756–7.   58 S. Heaney, *Redress of Poetry*, op. cit., p. 87. See also Heaney, 'Oscar Wilde Dedication: Westminster Abbey, 14 February 1995' in *Wilde the Irishman*, op. cit., p. 175. There he says that the ballad 'looks back to all the convict ballads, gaol journals and policial poetry of Irish nationalist literature in the nineteenth

men are not political prisoners. In fact Wilde changed the ugly scene of the original crime to give it a more Salometic tinge. Charles Thomas Wooldridge did not kill his wife in her bed: he slit her throat with a razor on a dark road one night, where he had been waiting for her.[59] But Wilde wanted the erotic charge of 'bed' right there at the beginning of the poem, dominating and determining the next 108 stanzas:

> And blood and wine were on his hands
> When they found him with the dead,
> The poor dead woman whom he loved,
> And murdered in her bed.[60]

The phrase 'her bed' keeps the crime in the private sphere, and the 'blood and wine' link the scene with the eroticized violence of *The Picture of Dorian Gray* or *Salomé*. Wooldridge enters the poem as a Wildean lover.

The crime of passion in 'The Ballad of Reading Gaol' remains a crime. As Regina Gagnier notes, Wilde's narrator 'does not complain that the punishment is unjust, but merely points out that it is indiscriminately applied'.[61] What drives the poem is Wilde's identification with the trooper, 'a figure through whom he could indulge in a vicarious exercise of self-castigation and self-pity', in Heaney's words.[62] As Wilde sees it, all the prisoners are as guilty as the trooper is, and yet it is only he who is hanged. At the moment of his execution, he lets out a scream, and Wilde says (punning on his name),

century'. In *Oscar Wilde: The Importance of Being Irish* (Dublin, 1994), Davis Coakley cites approvingly A.J. Leventhal's argument that Wilde drew on the Young Ireland poet Denis Florence McCarthy's poem 'A New Year's Song' when he wrote 'The Ballad of Reading Gaol' p. 210; and see Leventhal, 'Denis Florence McCarthy' in *Thomas Davis and Young Ireland 1845–1945*, ed. M.J. MacManus (Dublin, 1945), p. 106. Both Coakley and Leventhal argue that Wilde used the 'same metre' as McCarthy. But the stanza forms are not identical; see D.F. McCarthy, 'A New Year's Song', *The Spirit of the Nation* (Dublin, 1862), pp 190–1. The stanza form of 'Ballad of Reading Gaol' is, however, identical to that of 'The Walrus and the Carpenter'. Scholars arguing for Wilde's indebtedness to the Young Ireland poets also adduce his comments on that subject in remarks he delivered at Platt Hall in San Francisco in 1882. See M.J. O'Neill, 'Irish Poets of the Nineteenth Century: Unpublished Lecture Notes of Oscar Wilde', *University Review* 1.4 (Spring 1955), 29–32. **59** R. Ellmann, *Oscar Wilde*, op. cit., p. 472. **60** O. Wilde, 'The Ballad of Reading Gaol', *De Profundis and Other Writings* (London, 1986), p. 231. **61** R. Gagnier, *Idylls of the Marketplace: Oscar Wilde and the Victorian Public* (Stanford, 1986), p. 173. **62** S. Heaney, *Redress of Poetry*, op. cit., p. 89.

And all the woe that moved him so
    That he gave that bitter cry,
And the wild regrets, and the bloody sweats,
    None knew so well as I;
For he who lives more lives than one
    More deaths than one must die.[63]

'None knew so well' as the narrator the murderer's regrets and terrors; but, by implication, all the prisoners knew it in some degree. While establishing Wilde's identification with the trooper, the poem also establishes his 'allegiance to the community of prisoners'.[64] The first person plural of 'The Ballad of Reading Gaol' constitutes the transformation of the male community of the speech from the dock – Plato, Michelangelo, Shakespeare – into a potentially political group. The ballad marks another stage in Wilde's gradual politicization of male homosexuals and of homosexuality as a 'cause'. Yet even there, the nature of the speaker's 'wild regrets' remains a mystery and the name of his own passionate crime is never revealed. Slowly, gradually, after his release, Wilde began to speak with a different consciousness of the trial's meaning. Retrospectively, he shaped his experiences to fit the religious paradigm from which the Irish paradigm takes its shape: 'I shall now live as the Infamous St. Oscar of Oxford, Poet and Martyr', he wrote to Robbie Ross in 1898.[65] Just as, in Sinfield's analysis, 'notions' of the gay man had emerged around Wilde in the general culture after the trials, so they did in Wilde himself also. It was after the trial, then, and not in the dock, that he spoke about homosexuality as a cause. Discussing homophobia with Frank Harris, he said, 'I hold to my conviction – the best minds even now don't condemn us, and the world is becoming more tolerant'.[66] That 'us' is the transformed, politicized male community to which, in Gagnier's phrase, he now feels 'allegiance'. To George Ives he wrote, 'I have no doubt we shall win, but the road is long, and red with monstrous martyrdoms.'[67] To Ross he wrote in 1898, 'A patriot put in prison for loving his country loves his country, and a poet

63 O. Wilde, 'Ballad of Reading Gaol', op. cit., p. 243. 64 R. Gagnier, *Idylls of the Marketplace*, op. cit., p. 175. 65 Letter to Robert Ross [?18 March 1898], *Complete Letters*, op. cit., p. 1041. 66 F. Harris, *Oscar Wilde* (New York, 1992), p. 293. 67 Letter to George Ives [21 March 1898], *Complete Letters*, op. cit., p. 1044.

in prison for loving boys loves boys. To have altered my life would have been to have admitted that Uranian love is ignoble. I hold it to be noble – more noble than other forms.'[68]

There Paulin's and Eagleton's martyr seems to speak; but this is written three years after the trial, whereas in the dock he had denied erotic content to the 'Love that dare not speak its name'. Moreover, these hints and sketches of a system are fragmentary and piecemeal, emerging at particular moments when Wilde is provoked to politicize, not when he is creating ballads or scenarios. In the private genres of letters and conversations, in short, spontaneous forms not intended for publication, Wilde's love did dare speak its name: 'loving boys', 'Uranian love'. Clearly he was thinking of a collective 'we', a group whose long public struggle was just beginning: 'the road is long, and red with monstrous martyrdoms'. But even then, even flaunting the religious discourse central to Irish political martyrology, Wilde doesn't quite sound like Robert Emmet or the Manchester Martyrs. The larger context of one of the longer such passages indicates the tone and coloration of his thought. Speaking of William Ernest Henley's disparaging reviews of 'The Ballad of Reading Gaol', Wilde wrote Ross ('St Robert'),

> I am quite obliged to him for playing the role of the *Advocatus Diaboli* so well. Without it my beatification as a saint would have been impossible, but I shall now live as the Infamous St Oscar of Oxford, Poet and Martyr. My niche is just below that of the Blessed St Robert of Phillimore, Lover and Martyr – a saint known in *Hagiographia* for his extraordinary power, not in resisting, but in supplying temptation to others. This he did in the solitude of great cities, to which he retired at the comparatively early age of eight.[69]

This is martyrdom with a difference, a system devised by a mischievous, ludic sensibility. Wilde's private hagiographic system finds honorary titles for the friend who inducted him into homosexual practices, now canonized for 'supplying temptation to others', and for himself. Wilde the oppositional celebrity sounds like no one so much as his mother, amused by her own notoriety: 'if an illustrated history of Ireland is published no

68 Letter to Robert Ross [?18 February 1898], ibid., p. 1019. 69 See note 63.

doubt I shall be immortalized in the act of addressing the court.' Constructing the gay cathedral to express another kind of collective immortality, or hinting at such an edifice, Wilde places himself and his first male lover in neighbouring niches.

NOTE

I am grateful to Nicholas Grene for inviting me to speak at the Wilde Legacy symposium, Trinity College Dublin, December 2000, where the original version of this paper was delivered. Grateful thanks also to scholars who suggested valuable changes and additions: Robert Caserio, Declan Kiberd, Deirdre McMahon, Sally Mitchell, Yopie Prins.

'I see it is my *name* that terrifies': Wilde in the twentieth century

ALAN SINFIELD

NAMING THE UNSPEAKABLE

'I see it is my *name* that terrifies.' Many accounts of Wilde begin with his elaborate names. 'Others have names; I have a whole sentence,' Terry Eagleton's 'Saint Oscar' remarks: 'I was born with a sentence hanging over me.'[1] My theme in this essay is not how Oscar Fingal O'Flahertie Wills Wilde managed his given appellation, nor how he came to be called C.3.3., and then Sebastian Melmoth (a peculiar choice, I've always thought, for someone supposedly aiming to be inconspicuous). I want to consider how the name 'Oscar Wilde' circulated as a cultural icon in the twentieth century.

My title quotation is from a letter in which Wilde accepts, in 1898, that it might be wise to publish *The Ballad of Reading Gaol* anonymously in the United States: 'As regards America, I think it would be better now to publish there *without* my name. I see it is my *name* that terrifies.'[2] As a consequence of the trials, Wilde's name, which had previously signaled a complex bundle of attributes, became the term for something which had been hardly named hitherto. 'A detestable and abominable sin, amongst Christians not to be named', the jurist Sir Edward Coke had called it in 1644.[3] Casual uses echoed this judgment. 'The love he bore to Dan', Sir Henry Hall Caine wrote in 1887, 'was a brotherly passion for which language has yet no name'.[4] 'No one dares speak of it; or if they do, they bate their breath', wrote John Addington Symonds, 'surely it deserves a name.'[5]

1 T. Eagleton, *Saint Oscar* (Derry, 1989), p. 7. 2 R. Hart-Davis (ed.), *The Letters of Oscar Wilde* (New York, 1962), p. 698. 3 Quoted in B.R. Smith, *Homosexual Desire in Shakespeare's England: a cultural poetics* (Chicago, 1991), pp 49–51. 4 H.H. Caine, *The Deemster*, quoted in B. Reade, *Sexual Heretics: male homosexuality in English literature 1850–1900* (London, 1970), p. 208. 5 J.A. Symonds, *A Problem in Modern Ethics* (1891) in

Hence Lord Alfred Douglas' famous line about the love that dare not speak its name. However, one was about to be designated: 'Oscar Wilde'.

I got into working on Wilde as the first chapter of a book on lesbian and gay theatre in the twentieth century. Despite my attempts at brisk exposition, he proved unconfinable: the chapter grew into a book, *The Wilde Century*.[6] What struck me was this. For fourteen years, from his student days at Oxford until the trials in 1895, Wilde camped it up outrageously, first as an aesthete, then as a dandy. The question is not why he was harassed and prosecuted, but how he got away with it for so long. Even when the trials began, people such as W.B. Yeats and Frank Harris didn't believe the charges. Queensberry put into the witness box boys who said they had engaged in sexual acts with Wilde, but people thought he had been fitted up. This is my point: they didn't recognize Wilde *as a homosexual* because they didn't know what that unnamed creature looked like. They didn't know, as we do, that he looked like Oscar Wilde.

The unspeakable became synonymous with Wilde; he *became*, up into the mid-twentieth century and beyond, the dominant image of the male homosexual (mostly I am going to call him 'queer', using the informal language of the period). Before that date, to be sure, there were men who engaged in same-sex practices, and some of them had a concept of what they were doing. Some thought of themselves as mary-annes, effeminates, inverts, uranians, the third sex. Some of them were campy like Wilde. But at this point a distinctive image cohered, far more clearly, and for far more people than hitherto. Wilde's name – and with it the entire, vaguely disconcerting nexus of effeminacy, flamboyance, idleness, immorality, luxury, philandering, insouciance, leisure, decadence and aestheticism which he had cultivated – was transformed suddenly into a brilliantly precise image: the queer man. If you were queer yourself, or sympathetic, you called it 'camp'. 'These notes are for Oscar Wilde', Susan Sontag writes in her 'Notes on Camp'.[7]

M. Blasius and S. Phelan (eds), *We Are Everywhere: a historical sourcebook of gay and lesbian politics* (New York, 1997), p. 92. 6 See A. Sinfield, *The Wilde Century: effeminacy, Oscar Wilde and the Queer Moment* (London, New York, 1994); A. Sinfield, *Out on Stage: Lesbian and Gay Theatre in the Twentieth Century* (New Haven, 1999). 7 F. Cleto (ed.), *Camp: queer aesthetics and the performing subject: a reader* (Edinburgh, 1999), p. 54.

HOW TO KNOW ONE WHEN YOU SEE ONE

The author Beverley Nichols, as a boy in his teens during the First World War, was taken up by an effeminate aesthete who lived nearby. Nichols' biographer, Bryan Connon, tells how his father (a businessman) evidently 'assumed that the sophisticated Mr Edwards, who had a baronet in his family, was introducing Beverley to the world of the gentry. He never budged from his belief that [Edwards] was a hell of a fellow with the ladies' until Edwards gave young Beverley a copy of *The Picture of Dorian Gray*, and his father found him reading it. Mr Nichols went frantic: he called Beverley a ' "pretty little boy", enunciating the word "pretty" in a shrill parody of a homosexual voice as he hit him across the face. Then he spat on the book and tore the pages with his teeth. "Oscar Wilde! To think that my son ..." ' Edwards could still be perceived as a leisure-class phi-landerer, but he was transformed into a queer when the name of Wilde was uttered. 'The horrible crime which is not to be named', Mr Nichols called it.[8] Young Beverley was not put off, however; he became the first man at Oxford to wear suede shoes.[9]

The terror of Wilde's name was experienced across the classes. Robert Roberts, who grew up in Salford in Edwardian times, recalls it in his account of *The Classic Slum*:

> In pub and workshop there was plenty of talk, *sub rosa*, about the unspeakable. The working class, always fascinated by the great criminal trials, had been stirred to its depths by the prosecution of Oscar Wilde in 1895. As late as the first world war the ribald cry heard in factories, 'Watch out for oscarwile!' mystified raw young apprentices. The proletariat knew and marked what they consid-ered to be sure signs of homosexuality, though the term was unknown. Any evidence of dandyism in the young was severely frowned on ... any interest in music, books or the arts in general, learning or even courtesy and intelligence could make one suspect.[10]

8 B. Connon, *Beverley Nichols: a Life* (London, 1991), pp 39–40. 'The horrible crime which is not to be named' is Beverley's translation from Mr Nichols' Latin.   9 M. Green, *Children of the Sun* (London, 1977), pp 186–7.   10 R. Roberts, *The Classic Slum: Salford life in the first quarter of the century* (Manchester, 1971), pp 54–5.

Ed Cohen has noticed how Flora Thompson in *Lark Rise to Candleford* (1945) describes the impact of what she calls 'the tragedy of Oscar Wilde' on a rural community:

> There were vices, then, in the world which one had not hitherto heard of – vices which, even now, were only hinted at darkly, never described. Fathers for weeks and weeks kept the newspapers locked up with their account books. Mothers when appealed to for information shuddered and said in terrified accents: 'Never let me hear that name pass your lips again.'[11]

After a short break, Wilde's plays were performed again and *Reading Gaol* was set for learning in schools. Audiences and readers managed to dissociate the writer from the criminal – very much as they managed, for the most part, to overlook signals of queerness generally. But Wilde's notoriety was rekindled by scandals such as Robbie Ross's unsuccessful libel suit against Lord Alfred Douglas in respect of accusations of homosexuality (1914), and Maud Allan's unsuccessful suit against the fascistic Noel Pemberton Billing over his comments on her performance in Wilde's *Salomé* (1918). These cases turned on how far the accused and witnesses could be shown to be tainted by association with Wilde.[12]

The terrifying name figures time and again in mid-century biography, autobiography and oral history. T.E. Lawrence's mother would not have it mentioned by her undergraduate sons, especially in front of a girl.[13] John Betjeman, at school, 'discovered that Oscar Wilde was someone one ought not to mention; so naturally he had great attraction' for him. Betjeman wrote to Lord Alfred Douglas, but his father intercepted the replies and warned him off.[14] In the 1950s still, Paul Bailey recalls:

> 'Pansy' was the word my family used whenever the 'love that dare not speak its name' was spoken of, derisively. Oscar Wilde was

11 Quoted in E. Cohen, *Talk on the Wilde Side: towards a genealogy of a discourse on male sexualities* (New York, 1993), pp 100–1.   12 See P. Hoare, *Wilde's Last Stand: decadence, conspiracy and the First World War* (London, 1997).   13 See J.E. Mack, *A Prince of Our Disorder: the life of T.E. Lawrence* (Oxford, 1990), p. 10.   14 See H. David, *On Queer Street: a social history of British homosexuality, 1895–1995* (London, 1997), pp 31–2.

mentioned, too: 'He looks like an Oscar Wilde to me'; 'He's the Oscar Wilde type'; 'I know an Oscar Wilde when I see one'. These Oscar Wilde's were invariably famous, with their photographs in the papers – actors, principally; ballet dancers, painters, composers.[15]

Bailey's father was a road sweeper, his mother was in domestic service.

Two things are striking here. One is that queerness is supposed to be unspeakable, almost unknowable; yet there is sufficient awareness in all sectors of society for the name to trigger an immediate and vivid comprehension. Wilde anticipated this process in the letter which supplies my title quotation. The authorship of *The Ballad of Reading Gaol* would of course become known, he remarked: 'The public like an open secret.'[16] And so it was. All the reviewers of the poem knew that Wilde had written it, Richard Ellmann says, but none mentioned him by name.[17]

The other is that the Wildean image was even more influential among gay men than in society generally. A cult of Oscar Wilde, the 1890s and queerness became a way to express disengagement from establishment values in reaction to the First World War. Martin Green tells how Ronald Firbank and Harold Acton listened eagerly to Reggie Turner's stories of Wilde; Acton and Brian Howard appeared at the theatre 'in full evening dress, with long white gloves draped over one arm, and carrying silver-topped canes and top-hats, looking perhaps like a couple of Oscar Wildes'.[18] 'Wilde lived on', Philip Hoare observes, 'in the literary antics of the Sitwells, the neo-baroque stylism of Cecil Beaton and Rex Whistler, and in the truly Firbankian figure of the androgynous Stephen Tennant'.[19]

Other gay men acknowledged but resisted the Wildean image. E.M. Forster's eponymous Maurice knows no other way to name himself than as 'an unspeakable of the Oscar Wilde sort'.[20] Indeed, the novel has a Wildean character, the aristocratic Risley, but Maurice is not actually like that. Gay men, Forster wants to show, need not be Wildean effeminates. Again, the journalist Michael Davidson thought of himself as a more mas-

15 P. Bailey, *An Immaculate Mistake* (London, 1990), pp 93–4. **16** R. Hart-Davis, *Letters*, op. cit., p. 698. **17** R. Ellmann, *Oscar Wilde* (London, 1987), p. 526. **18** M. Green, *Children of the Sun*, op. cit., p. 115. **19** P. Hoare, *Wilde's Last Stand*, op. cit., p. 227. **20** E.M. Forster, *Maurice* (London, 1972), p. 139.

culine type, but at the age of eighteen 'still vaguely believed that I and Oscar Wilde ... were the only people since the age of Alkibiades to be *born* with this yearning'. And someone he met at a swimming pool in Southampton.[21]

After the Second World War the open secret became a subject of public debate in England: the Wolfenden Committee was appointed in 1954 and reported in 1957 (its recommendations were largely adopted in the law of 1967). Wilde became very visible in print, on stage and on screen, in biographical and critical commentary.[22] Peter Wildeblood, who had been made infamous by another trial – of himself and Lord Montagu in 1954 – complained:

> I suppose that most people, if they were asked to define the crime of Oscar Wilde, would still imagine that he was an effeminate poseur who lusted after small boys, whereas in fact he was a married man with two small children ... In every generation there have probably been hundreds of adolescents who have been first puzzled, and then unwholesomely fascinated by the aura of secrecy and sordid glamour which still surrounds the case ... since Wilde is probably the best-known of homosexuals, it is supposed that all of them share the tendencies which have, quite wrongly as it happens, been ascribed to him.[23]

Gay Liberation, in England and the United States from around 1970, did not make obsolete the debates around Wilde. Angus Wilson told me how he was invited to a gay youth group: 'What was it like, knowing Oscar Wilde?' they asked. In particular, the potential of camp as a subversive discourse has been argued around him. Jonathan Dollimore counterposes the strategic arguments and self-presentation of Wilde and Gide. Wilde exemplifies anti-essentialism – subverting through camp the categories that aspire to contain transgression; Gide exemplifies essentialism – appropriating the natural, the normal, the authentic. 'Whereas for Wilde transgressive desire leads to a relinquishing of the essential self, for Gide it

21 Michael Davidson, *The World, the Flesh and Myself* (London, 1977), p. 80.   22 For a list see A. Sinfield, *The Wilde Century*, op. cit., p. 143.   23 P. Wildeblood, *Against the Law* (London, 1955), pp 5–6.

leads to its discovery.'[24] Gregory Bredbeck poses the question again in Moe Meyer's collection, *The Politics and Poetics of Camp*: 'Why has gay male culture embraced Wilde *as* Camp and Camp *as* political?'[25]

Wilde is not going away. In the film *Four Weddings and Funeral* (1994) the flamboyant gay character played by Simon Callow is asked if he knows Oscar Wilde. In Todd Haynes' film *Velvet Goldmine* (1998) Wilde is invoked as the inspiration for the stardom, exoticism, decadence, queerness and ultimate integrity of 1970s Glam-Rock.

AS ENGLISH AS MORRIS DANCING

How far and in what ways the dissemination of the Wildean queer images might apply to Ireland needs a lot more investigation. Of course, Irish culture has Roger Casement to cope with as well; as pertinently as when Yeats made the point, 'The ghost of Roger Casement / Is beating on the door'.[26] Padraic Pearse seems to echo *The Ballad of Reading Gaol* in his homoerotic play *The Master*: 'a man shall not find his quest unless he kill the dearest thing he has.'[27] The young Brendan Behan in *Borstal Boy* finds a queer circle, centred upon a boy who sports a cigarette holder and a rose coloured silk tie and is reading Harris' *Life of Oscar Wilde*.[28] The scholar and critic Éibhear Walshe records that for him Wilde has performed an iconic function. Walshe has encountered two problems, however. One is that Wilde's writing was 'mainly light and frothy, Coward-like in its luminous, delicate irrelevancy'; these are the familiar limitations of Wildean queerness. The second problem is that Wilde 'seemed to be more English than Irish in his writing'.[29]

---

24 J. Dollimore, *Sexual Dissidence: Augustine to Wilde, Freud to Foucault* (Oxford, 1991), p. 13.   **25** G. W. Bredbeck, 'Narcissus in the Wilde: Textual Cathexis and the Historical Origins of Queer Camp' in M. Meyer (ed.), *The Politics and Poetics of Camp* (London, 1994), pp 51–74, at p. 52. See also F. Cleto (ed.), *Camp*, op. cit.   **26** 'The Ghost of Roger Casement' in *The Collected Poems of W.B. Yeats* (London, 1950), p. 352.   **27** P.H. Pearse, *Plays, Stories, Poems* (Dublin, 1980), p. 90.   **28** B. Behan, *Borstal Boy* (London, 1990), pp 243–4. I owe this and the previous instance to Vincent Quinn. See his article 'Patrick Pearse, Catholicism, and Intergeneration Desire', forthcoming.   **29** É. Walshe, 'Oscar's Mirror' in Í. O'Carroll and E. Collins (eds), *Lesbian and Gay Visions of Ireland: towards the 21st Century* (London, 1995), pp 147–57, at pp 147–9. See É. Walshe (ed.), *Sex, Nation and Dissent in Irish Writing* (Cork, 1997).

The fact that so much of Wilde's notoriety appears to be situated in England has licensed commentators to avoid pondering such matters in an Irish context. Students at Oxford, Eagleton found, didn't even know that Wilde was Irish.[30] (I daresay they didn't know Terry was either.) More strikingly, Jerusha McCormack reports, students at University College Dublin didn't know that Wilde was born in Dublin, holidayed in the West and studied at Trinity College.[31] Of course, this has not been an accidental forgetting. For how can Wilde's Irishness be addressed without including his queerness?

The answer is: more readily than might have been supposed. McCormack's *Wilde the Irishman* is one of several recent volumes reclaiming Wilde as the Irish genius who was misled and betrayed by the English whom he rashly courted and derided. However, the essays collected by McCormack, apart from her own introduction, have little to say about queerness. Might Wilde not have begun his deviant career at Portora School? No, Owen Dudley Edwards assures us, 'there is not the slightest reason to believe that Portora proved its Englishness as a public school by introducing Wilde to homosexuality'.[32] Queerness is English, to the point where even an Irish school that cultivated English principles could not have kindled it. Again: Wilde's tutor at Trinity, Dr John Mahaffy, is hardly mentioned by McCormack's contributors, and no one broaches his progressive views on Greek homosexuality, which he published in 1874 in his book *Social Life in Greece from Homer to Meander*. 'As to the epithet *unnatural*, the Greeks would answer probably, that all civilisation was unnatural', Mahaffy declares. He acknowledges Wilde's help in 'making improvements and corrections all through the book'.[33] One might have expected this courageous and progressive work to be a matter of pride, and Wilde's association with it to be worth discussing.

Another volume, *Rediscovering Oscar Wilde*, edited by C. George Sandulescu, is published in The Princess Grace Irish Library, in the wake

---

30 T. Eagleton, *Saint Oscar*, op. cit., p. vii. 31 J. McCormack, 'Introduction: The Irish Wilde' in McCormack (ed.), *Wilde the Irishman* (New Haven, 1998), pp 1–5, at p. 5. 32 O. Dudley Edwards, 'Impressions of an Irish Sphinx' in *Wilde the Irishman*, op. cit., pp 47–71, at p. 67. Edwards does allow that other Portora graduates were 'infinitely more proficient from earliest adolescence in the sexual expression universally associated with Oscar Wilde' p. 67. 33 Quoted in R. Ellmann, *Oscar Wilde*, op. cit., pp 27–8.

of collections on Yeats and Joyce. Sexuality is hardly mentioned; Mahaffy's witty conversation figures (he wrote a book on that too), but not his account of Greek sexuality.[34] Davis Coakley in his biography, *Oscar Wilde: The Importance of Being Irish*, cites Mahaffy on the Greeks, but finds it unnecessary to refer to Wilde's sexuality until the eve of the trials.[35] In Ireland too, I infer, his name has borne an element of terror.

Richard Pine's stated project, in his courageous study *The Thief of Reason*, is to show 'the interchangeability of homosexuality and Irishness as ways of seeing and thinking and ways of being seen and being described'. Yet even Pine presents queerness as something an Irishman might encounter on arrival in England: 'At Oxford Wilde brought the Irish personality into an arena where homosexuality, religion and aesthetics were earnestly discussed.'[36] Denis Donoghue queries but doesn't quite repudiate allegations by Yeats and Q. D. and F. R. Leavis, that Oxford inspired Wilde's capitulation to a debilitating, homosocial and passive 'feminine charm'.[37] Again, queerness seems to start in England.

'You are a bugger, Mr Wilde, are you not?' Carson accuses in Eagleton's *Saint Oscar*.

> Not at all, sir; I am Irish. There are no buggers in Ireland; the Church would not allow it. We are a God-fearing people, pious to a fault; we even dance chastely, arms pinned to sides. We are also one of the most sexually prolific nations in the world. Simple arithmetic will indicate that Irish sodomites must be unusually thin on the ground.

Queerness, conversely, is English. 'I am accused of homosexual relations by an Establishment for whom such practices are as habitual as high tea. Homosexual behaviour is as English as morris dancing, if somewhat less tedious. To try a man in this country for homosexuality is as illogical as trying him for foxhunting', Eagleton's Wilde declares.[38]

---

34 C. George Sandulescu (ed.), *Rediscovering Oscar Wilde* (Gerrards Cross, 1994). 35 D. Coakley, *Oscar Wilde: The Importance of Being Irish* (Dublin, 1994), pp 156–8, 206–9. 36 R. Pine, *The Thief of Reason: Oscar Wilde and Modern Ireland* (Dublin, 1995), pp 415, 129. Pine does refer to Mahaffy on Greek sexuality, pp 125–6. 37 D. Donoghue, 'The Oxford of Pater, Hopkins, and Wilde' in *Rediscovering Oscar Wilde*, op. cit., pp 94–117, at pp 112–16. 38 T. Eagleton, *Saint Oscar*, op. cit., pp 35, 40.

The notion that sexual perversion is one of the impositions of an impe-rial power is not uncommon in nationalist movements; scandals were exposed at Dublin Castle, the seat of English governance, by Home Rule campaigners in the 1880s and 1900s.[39] On the other hand, cultures found-ed in resistance to a colonial oppression may be sensitive to the oppres-sion of minorities (we see this in the South African leadership). In fact the Irish gay roll of honour has a notably radical slant. Walshe invokes Roger Casement, Eva Gore-Booth, Padraic Pearse, Brendan Behan and Kate O'Brien; Kieran Rose lists also Somerville and Ross and Forrest Reid.[40] Other bold figures include the Ladies of Llangollen, Neil Jordan (hon-orary, for *The Crying Game*), Emma Donoghue ... Stephen Gately. I don't need to dwell upon the controversies that have surrounded these people; of course, they make them more pertinent, not less.

In more hospitable reflections on Wilde's sexuality, for instance by Mc-Cormack and Seamus Heaney, it is implied that queerness, properly under-stood, may fade into a general postmodern indeterminacy; these names, these categories, are too unstable to matter any more.[41] Declan Kiberd per-ceives Wilde as a shape-changer, a name-changer – one not interested in def-inite identities. 'Inversion' for him was less to do with sexuality than with dislike of 'the manic Victorian urge to antithesis', and hence with 'a pro-found scorn for the extreme Victorian division between male and female'.[42] That may be true, and probably we should describe Wilde as bisexual rather than gay. But he liked boys to the point where he risked destruction: he did, at a common-sense level, rely on a divide between male and female.

To be sure, sexuality is not a fixed entity, either in an individual or in a culture. Nonetheless, a postmodern idea of Wilde (and everything else) as endlessly elusive can obscure the real determinants in cultural change. Twentieth-century uses of Wilde's name, certainly, have depended on sim-plifications, mistaken apprehensions and downright falsehoods. However, the point is not Wilde's true identity, but the identity that the trials foist-

39 See H.M. Hyde, *The Other Love: an historical and contemporary survey of homosexuality in Britain* (London, 1972), pp 146–52, 175–7.   40 É. Walshe, 'Oscar's Mirror', op. cit., pp 150–5; K. Rose, *Diverse Communities: the evolution of gay and lesbian politics in Ireland* (Cork, 1994), p. 9.   41 See J. McCormack, 'Introduction: The Irish Wilde' in *Wilde the Irishman*, op. cit., p. 2; S. Heaney, 'Oscar Wilde Dedication: Westminster Abbey, 14 February 1995', ibid., pp 174–6, at p. 175.   42 D. Kiberd, *Inventing Ireland* (London, 1995), pp 38–9.

ed on to him. It is not who he was, but who we have made him to be. I want to suggest that there is unfinished business here; that Ireland, as much as England and the United States, might claim the name of Wilde as a gay icon.

ACTOR AND RACKETEER

As I have said, the Wildean image of the homosexual could be a mixed blessing. One who seized upon it with enthusiasm was Alfred Willmore, who was born in 1899 to English parents in Kensal Green, West London (disconcertingly close to Wormwood Scrubs). His father was a broker in a company that supplied hay for horses. Christopher Fitz-Simon, his biographer, links Alfred Willmore indelibly with the manners and concerns of the 1890s: 'he admitted throughout his life that he should have been born thirty years earlier: he was a late arrival at the feast of J.K. Huysmans, Max Beerbohm and Oscar Wilde'. He studied art at the Slade School, preferring the style of Charles Ricketts, Arthur Rackham and Aubrey Beardsley. 'He should have submitted his work to the *Yellow Book*', Fitz-Simon adds.[43] He lived with his partner, Hilton Edwards, from 1927 until his death in 1978 (they both had other affairs as well); it was widely assumed that they were a couple. They got by on the open-secret pattern of knowledge, discretion and disavowal that attended the name of Wilde. Also, it was supposed, you have to put up with an element of queerness with these theatre types.

What is peculiarly apposite to my theme is that Willmore didn't only want to be queer on the Wildean model; he wanted to be Irish. During the First World War, in his late teens, he reinvented himself as Micheál MacLiammóir. He learnt Gaelic, became a Catholic, moved to Dublin, said he hailed from Cork. For the rest of his life he passed as Irish; there was gossip about his name, but only in 1990 was this given serious credence.[44] So while Wilde moved to England and affected English manners, to the point where his Irishness has been questioned, MacLiammóir moved in the other direction. While Wilde lost control of his name in

43 C. Fitz-Simon, *The Boys: a double biography* (London, 1994), p. 16.   44 Ibid., pp 70, 88.

England, MacLiammóir manipulated his to become whom he wanted in Ireland.

As Irish readers well know, he and Edwards founded the Dublin Gate Theatre in 1928 and for fifty years produced an astonishing range of Irish and international drama. MacLiammóir acted (he had begun his career as a child actor, alongside the equally young and seductive Noel Coward), Edwards managed and directed. They took Gate work to other Irish theatres, London, New York and all round the world. MacLiammóir was awarded the Douglas Hyde Award for Gaelic writing, the Lady Gregory Medal of the Irish Academy of Letters, and an honorary Doctor in Laws at Trinity College; he and Edwards were made Freemen of the City of Dublin.

Whether all this means that MacLiammóir may count as Irish is, thankfully, not for me to say. He is not indexed in Kiberd's *Inventing Ireland*, though we might say he was more inventive than most; 'Sodom and Begorrah, or Game to the Last: Inventing Micheál MacLiammóir' is the neat title of Walshe's essay on him.[45] But if we are all postmodern now and identities constitute questions rather than answers, then MacLiammóir offers an intriguing case.

The Gate produced Wilde's plays repeatedly, including in the first season, in 1928, *Salomé* (which was banned in England); they did MacLiammóir's dramatization of *Dorian Gray*. MacLiammóir initiated (in the face of opposition) the campaign for a plaque on the house where Wilde was born; he played Wilde in an English television reconstruction of the trials. Above all, for my purposes and for his own renown, he wrote and played, initially in 1960, a one-man show: *The Importance of Being Oscar*. This performance of the story of Wilde, with lengthy quotations and elegant commentary, started life at the Gate but was quickly taken up for the West End, Broadway, and extensive international tours over several years. I saw it, I think at the Royal Court in London in 1962.

MacLiammóir in his monologue admits no doubt of Wilde's Irishness. His move to England is not a difficulty: 'the one ordinary thing Oscar Wilde seems to have done in his life was to have fled away from his native Ireland as soon as he possibly could' – 'everybody was doing it'. In fluent

45 É. Walshe, 'Sodom and Begorrah, or Game to the Last: Inventing Michael MacLiammoir [*sic*]', in Walshe (ed.), *Sex, Nation and Dissent in Irish Writing*, op. cit., pp 150–69.

and witty Dublin his ability to talk would not have been specially prized, whereas he shone in 'wealthy, good-natured, tongue-tied England'.[46] The amusing symmetry, whereby MacLiammóir had himself relocated from England and was, in his own person on the stage, delivering Wilde back to Dublin, was known only to a handful of people. But it is there for us. So is another partly private joke about language and belonging, when MacLiammóir remarks of Wilde's warder, Tom Martin: he was 'from Belfast, our Northern capital, where they speak the English tongue with a very strange accent' (*Importance*, p. 56).

The version MacLiammóir gives of Wilde's sexuality is closeted in the extreme. He dwells upon Wilde's heterosexual relations, declaring that he was in love (successively) with Lily Langtry and with his wife; in 1895, still, he was a happy husband. No reason for Queensberry's objection is suggested; the insulting words with which he precipitated the trials ('To Oscar Wilde, posing somdomite') are not quoted; all we get is: 'on the card his Lordship had scribbled a few libelous and, incidentally, wrongly spelt words' (*Importance*, pp 44–5). This is noticeably slanted: 'libelous' implies that the words were false, whereas – the trials showed – they were substantially true; the comment on spelling bolsters the notion that the charge cannot warrant serious attention.

What makes it difficult for the audience of MacLiammóir's play to assess the scope of Wilde's sexual adventures is that the trials, in their entirety, occur *during the interval*! So there are no witnesses, no indictment, no defence, no cross-examination; no performance of Wilde's climactic speech – the love that dare not speak its name remains silent. Part two, after the interval, begins with the judge's sentence for a crime whose nature has not been specified, and dwells upon Wilde's redemption through Christian humility in *De Profundis* and *The Ballad of Reading Gaol*. MacLiammóir contrives to quote *De Profundis* so as to suggest that Wilde could have established his innocence if he had not chosen to protect the reputation of Douglas (*Importance*, pp 52–3).

Alongside this reluctance to admit that Wilde might have done anything improper, MacLiammóir conveys a strong sense of the terror that has lurked around his name. The tragedy, he tells the audience, is that 'to

46 M. MacLiammóir, *The Importance of Being Oscar* (Gerrards Cross, 1995), pp 16–17. Cited hereafter as *Importance*.

so many thousands of people today, the name of Oscar Wilde merely conjures up an immediate image of shame and scandal' (*Importance*, p. 48). The concluding thought in *The Importance of Being Oscar* is that slowly, after Wilde's death, 'his name, which for so many years had remained silent in the world, or was spoken only in shameful or bawdy whispers ... his name began once more to sound like a bell in the world of Art and Letters' (*Importance*, p. 70).

There is no pretending that this version of Wilde's sexuality, as redeemed through art and suffering, anticipates the Gay Liberation Front. The films starring Peter Finch and Robert Morley, also from 1959–60, are far more candid. As with Coward, MacLiammóir's training in discretion went back to his earliest experiences as a boy actor. He was actually introduced to Lord Alfred Douglas: 'You knew Oscar Wilde, didn't you?' he innocently enquired. There was, Fitz-Simon records, 'a startled silence followed by eager and animated conversation on every other topic imaginable'.[47]

Evidently, despite and because of its discretion, *The Importance of Being Oscar* depends on audience awareness of the mid-century pattern of knowledge and disavowal around Wilde's name which I have demonstrated in England. MacLiammóir wondered on occasion whether audiences were picking up all the references: when he quoted Wilde's letter comparing Douglas to Hyacinth, Jonquil and Narcissus, they 'might be wondering if he were referring to Woolworth's catalogues of spring bulbs'.[48] Very possibly. But the play assumes that they would know that Wilde had indulged a scandalous passion for the delicate young aristocrat, and that this could be spoken of only obliquely.

This knowledge was transmitted also by MacLiammóir's notoriously queenly presence. *The Importance of Being Oscar* displays the Wildean premises by which MacLiammóir had lived: exuding queerness in his every gesture while leaving its underlying disgrace unspoken.

The resemblance of Wilde and MacLiammóir is stressed by Edwards in his introduction to the published play text. 'It is as a biographer and a wit in his own right, as well as an actor, that MacLiammóir holds the stage ... As much as an actor he is an entertainer; a raconteur'.[49] (In Cleveland,

47 C. Fitz-Simon, *The Boys*, op. cit., p. 227. 48 Ibid., p. 239. 49 H. Edwards, 'Introduction to MacLiammóir', *The Importance of Being Oscar*, pp 5, 7.

Ohio, a columnist described MacLiammóir as 'actor and *racketeer*'; I'm told this is a significant slip.[50] 'His clouded-velvet voice, his exceptional capacity for appreciation, his gaiety and ready wit, all tend to make him a spell-binder' – like Wilde. And his performance is the kind of thing Wilde did – not just a recital, nor a lecture, but 'a full-length portrait in pre-Raphaelite detail, such as Wilde himself tells us was painted of Dorian Gray'.[51]

Furthermore, according to Edwards, these gifts locate Wilde and MacLiammóir in an Irish tradition: 'The *Seanchaí*, the story-teller, is a fast vanishing figure in the tradition of Gaelic and Irish culture. Oscar Wilde, though possibly unaware of it, owed much of his influence both as an artist and as a social lion to the craft of the *Seanchaí*.' And so with MacLiammóir.[52] In fact, MacLiammóir *is* Wilde, in his artistry, his sexuality, his nation, his camp manner; in all his complexity, he signals the affinity, under the name of Wilde, of queerness and Irishness. What we would like to know now is whether other, less famous Irishmen presented themselves in Wildean manner, and how their contemporaries regarded them. It is time for research on these topics.

The opportunity MacLiammóir was seeking to embody is for Ireland to share with England that substantial segment of gay history which Wilde had been made to designate. This potential has been invoked by Neil Sammells, who suggests that we may regard Wilde's green carnation buttonhole as 'the badge of a homosexual coterie, a demonstration of the self-consciously modern and refined taste which prefers the artificial to the natural, and a declaration of national allegiance which refracts and politicizes both'.[53] Wilde the Irishman and the aesthete is, by the same token, Wilde the queer. Pine too, cultivating a slippage between Yeatsian and sexual meanings of 'gay', posits a crucial overlap between Irish and queer attributes: 'It was his Irishness which for so long prevented all but his closest associates – even perhaps his wife –from detecting his homosexuality, because the two referential contexts were so proximate'.[54] Camp style was sufficiently like Irish style, in other words, to enable Wilde to pass.

50 C. Fitz-Simon, *The Boys*, op. cit., p. 250. 51 H. Edwards, 'Introduction', op. cit., pp 7, 9.
52 Ibid. 53 N. Sammells, 'Rediscovering the Irish Wilde' in *Rediscovering Oscar Wilde*, op. cit.,
pp 362–70, at p. 363. 54 R. Pine, *Thief of Reason*, op. cit., p. 12. On 'gay' see Pine's section on
'The Gay Temper' (pp 38–46) and Yeats's poems 'Lapis Lazuli' and 'Under Ben Bulben'.

These comments are compatible with MacLiammóir's argument about why Wildean *élan* would shine more brightly in England: in Ireland his fluent and witty conversation would merely incite competition, whereas 'wealthy, good-natured, tongue-tied England' would be impressed.[55] MacLiammóir is proffering Wilde's flamboyant, sophisticated manner – which gays recognise as camp – as typically Irish. The Wildean queer, as MacLiammóir found in his own life, may be at home in Dublin.

There is an heroic Irish-queer moment in *The Importance of Being Oscar*, though it is characteristically muted. While, as I have observed, MacLiammóir avoids quoting anything from the trials, he does fasten upon Wilde's question after sentence: 'And I? May I say nothing, my lord?' Suppose he had been allowed to speak, MacLiammóir wonders. 'Would he have delivered from the dock some speech comparable in eloquence and power to that of the Irish rebel leader Robert Emmet: a speech that, independently of his own fate, might have revealed the strange and uniquely Anglo-Saxon quality of the law that had sentenced him?' (*Importance*, p. 48). The speech MacLiammóir would have liked to perform would have exposed the oppressive character of English legislation on sexuality and linked Wilde with the insurrectionary Irish hero. It is not queerness that is peculiarly English, then, as seems to be the view of some of the commentators I discussed earlier, but a stodgy and irrational phobia about queerness; whereas revolutionary Ireland can incorporate dissident sexuality into its epic project. There wasn't much promise of that in 1960, but since 1993 the law on sexuality has been a good deal more advanced in the Republic than in England, Wales, Scotland and the six counties. For this we have specially to thank Senator David Norris. Even more distinctively, Rose observes, these reforms were enacted in an affirmative, rather than a grudging spirit.[56] Sadly, the wish of lesbians and gay men to parade on St Patrick's Day in Boston and New York remains controversial.

Once more: if the Wildean model of the queer man is a rightful part of Irish inheritance, that does not mean that this is what Irish gays must be like. To the contrary, as in England, the Wildean legacy is there to be recovered, contested and negotiated. It is a tool for thinking with, not an identity to be adopted.

55 M. MacLiammóir, *Importance of Being Oscar*, op. cit., pp 16–17. 56 See K. Rose, *Diverse Communities*, op. cit., pp 2–3.

If we hadn't had Wilde, we would have invented him; indeed, we did invent him! I don't apologise for this; it is how culture works, and we are not finished yet. I was involved in a television film – *A Fear to Appear Queer, Oscar Dear!* This was made by the BBC 2 Community and Disablement Unit in April 1995. People stopped me in the street to talk about it. A common line was: I've got nothing against you people, but why do you have to drag in Oscar Wilde? The reply, I realized, is: But we didn't. Wilde was doing his own thing, when the straight system insulted him, bankrupted him, took away his children, imprisoned him, exiled him. He was made to change his name, while his original name was co-opted to bespeak our unspeakableness. It is the English establishment that made Oscar Wilde a problem for gay people – as for Irish people. Now, by reviewing that history, we are making his name speak for us.

Index

Index